THE ENGL

The English Spirit

A New Approach

through

the World Conception

of

RUDOLF STEINER

D. E. FAULKNER JONES

LONDON
RUDOLF STEINER PRESS

First edition 1935
Second edition 1982

ISBN 05440 388 4 (cloth)
      05440 389 2 (paperback)

Printed and bound in Great Britain at
The Camelot Press Ltd, Southampton

CONTENTS

INTRODUCTION

The English Spirit was first published in 1935 by the Rudolf Steiner Press under its then name of Anthroposophical Publishing Co. Its author D. E. Faulkner Jones was a teacher of English in Manchester High School for Girls. That she was gifted with a vigorous and original mind hardly needs emphasising, since anyone who reads this Introduction may be assumed to be about to read, or perhaps to have read, the book. But some readers may like to know that, in addition to her profound feeling for and knowledge of English literature, and her extensive acquaintance with Rudolf Steiner's teachings in their historical and cosmological aspects (Anthroposophy), she was particularly concerned with the sociological side of those teachings, which had found expression after World War I in the Threefold Commonwealth Movement in Germany and in books such as *The Threefold Commonwealth* that arose out of it. She was an active member of a "Threefold Commonwealth Research Group", which flourished for some years in England during the '30s.

At first sight it may be felt that in going back to 1935, four years before the outbreak of World War II, we are entering a different world; and that accordingly a book that contains social and political observations as well as wide-ranging reflections on less transient phenomena must necessarily be out of date in 1982. But on closer acquaintance any such objection falls to the ground. There are all too many resemblances between the two worlds.

The outstanding feature of post-war life is the way in which facts, definite concrete events, have grown beyond the compass of human will. For instance, there has never been a time in the history of man when individual human beings have so ardently and consciously desired peace: yet the world is bristling with armaments, and militaristic passions are stirring in the breasts of men, each of whom would nevertheless receive with genuine indignation the suggestion that he personally was anxious to plunge the world into blood. Against the wishes, against the reason, against the moral judgment, of the vast majority of the individuals composing it, the world is drifting, like a rudderless ship, towards the abyss.

It would take a very rash optimist to deny that the above description from chapter 1 is more, not less, true if "post-war" is taken to refer to World War II and not—as it in fact does—to the 1914–18 War.

More generally, any remark to the effect that a book "dates" should be examined very carefully before it is accepted. If it refers to the ideas in the book, it is no more than a worthless cliché reflecting the shallow, but very prevalent notion that, because an idea is outmoded it is on that account discredited. It is another matter of course if the book refers to too many ephemeral events, or topics no longer within the scope of an average reader's knowledge of the world. Apart from the reference to C. H. Douglas in the final chapter, on which I have added a note at the end of this Introduction, I find no such references in *The English Spirit*. On the other hand the glib assumption that what is past is of no importance is one of the symptoms of that very disease which Faulkner Jones attacks so valiantly in her book: ". . . the rapid changes of modern life are tending to cut us off from our own past: we ourselves are beginning to allow our spiritual heritage to slip out of our grasp, and if the present trend of evolution continues, there will soon arise in England a generation to whom the works of her noblest writers will be sealed books." Since those words were written another generation *has* arisen. And what is its intellectual climate? Brief and brittle thoughts hurriedly stuffed into empty heads to allay the pangs, with the media growing more and more efficient every year at keeping up the supply. The philosophy behind it all, if there is one, is the ass of chronological parochialism in the lion's skin of a gaze sternly averted from the past and fixed bravely on the future.

It is against this sort of light-mindedness that the author sets her concept of a "spiritual heritage". And, being herself English, it is the spiritual heritage of England with which she is mainly concerned; of England, as she more than once emphasises, not "Britain" or the British Empire. The year 1935 came at the beginning of the period during which England has been steadily relinquishing, or as it has turned out, dismantling, her empire. Whether that was wise or unwise, or whether it was done too hurriedly, is not here in issue. Before it began to be done our author had made up her mind, as G. K. Chesterton and others had done before her, that the Great Britain of the Empire had little to do with the spiritual heritage of England and was, if anything, a threat to it. What then is this so-called spiritual heritage? The answer to that question, as the author saw it, lies in the book itself and there is no need for me to try and anticipate it. But notice that it is a question which admits of two different, though complementary, answers, a short-term and a long-term one. The short-term one, measured let us say in centuries, involves consideration of English Literature and Art (on which the main attention of the book is focused), of her political and religious development, her social mores, the special quality of the patriotism she can invoke and so forth. It was Faulkner Jones's express reliance on the insights and findings of Rudolf Steiner that enabled her to supplement, and indeed permeate, all this with the long-term concept of a spiritual heritage, measured in millennia and aeons.

This is made clear in the opening paragraphs. And here let me remark that her book has to my mind the additional merit of affording an example of the sort of contribution to the growing literature of Anthroposophy that is all too rare.

> The views put forward by the writer are purely personal, and are not intended to be taken in any narrow, dogmatic sense. They have arisen from a union of concepts derived from Steiner's teaching and the results not only of personal observation and experience, but of attempts to study English Literature as an Imaginative picture of spiritual realities.
>
> Those who can accept as rational Rudolf Steiner's teaching that Germany is the representative of the universal Ego, while England represents the individualised Ego. . . .
>
> The aim of the following studies is limited and comparatively simple: the writer has taken from Steiner's work certain definite ideas and has sought to illustrate them, to give them a richer content, by showing how they fit in with facts well-known to English people. . . . Readers will thus be able to judge for themselves whether, within this limited sphere, Steiner's thought can throw new light on the problems of modern life.

These are only selected examples of her "stance" (as

the Americans like to say). And it is very much the
stance which Steiner himself wished to see adopted
towards his writings. Think my thoughts without
believing or disbelieving them; apply them to an area
you know well; and see if they illumine it. The author
of *The English Spirit* found them throwing a fresh light
on much with which she was familiar, from the
enclosed tranquillity, the *hortus conclusus*, into which
Jane Austen's novels transport us to the austerities and
sublimities of Shakespeare's *Hamlet* and *King Lear*. On
King Lear in particular they enabled her, for myself at
all events, to write the best kind of criticism there is—
the kind that keeps making you doubt for a moment
whether you ever really read the play before. I could
say pretty much th e same about her long analysis of
Tennyson's *In Memoriam* in Chapter III. As to the
briefer and more passing touches of luminous comment, such as the contrast between Goethe's *Wilhelm
Meister* and Boswell's *Life of Johnson* in the same
chapter. I could no doubt swell this Introduction by
searching them out and listing them, but I prefer to
leave the sensitive reader to discover them for himself
and return instead to the central theme of the book,
England's "spiritual heritage".

The book begins with a brief account of Steiner's
triune psychology, including an explanation of what is
meant by the term "Spiritual Soul" and of its peculiar
relation to England and the history of England. (It is
by the way a little surprising that the author nowhere
mentions its other label, "Consciousness Soul", though
Steiner in fact used it more frequently, and it points to
the heart of her matter.) She continues:

Two important, and apparently contradictory, ideas frequently occur in Rudolf Steiner's work. On the one hand he regarded England, the representative of the Spiritual Soul, as the true source of that materialism which has spread like a blight over Europe and is now attacking the East with great power. And, on the other hand, he admitted that the English people themselves have somehow escaped the worst consequences of the materialism they have generated. They have poisoned others, while themselves remaining comparatively uninjured. . . . It is nothing short of tragic that the rest of the world should assimilate the materialistic and utilitarian elements in English life, while misunderstanding and rejecting its loftiest spirituality.

In musical parlance this might be called the opening unadorned statement of her theme: the notion of two Englands, the exterior and the interior, the body and the soul. For whether she speaks of the spiritual heritage or of "the Soul of England" it is in effect the same thing she is referring to It is these which she finds manifested respectively in the England of the Industrial Revolution and of scientific and technological hegemony, and at its opposite pole in the England of "the humanities", with which her book is mainly concerned. It hardly affects her argument, though it may affect (and not necessarily adversely) our chances of profiting by it, that the hegemony had already declined substantially between Steiner's day and her own, and during the period since her book was published has been transferred to Germany, Japan and the United States. It is of course the same polar contrast which underlies her sharp distinction between the "Great Britain" of nineteenth-century chauvinism and the England of Chaucer, Shakespeare, Milton and their successors in title—or, at a lower level, of Bully

Bottom, Dick Swiveller and Mr. Pickwick. Others, as I have remarked, have felt something the same about this, including no doubt some of the unpopular "little Englanders" of Boer War days. But I do not know that anyone else has related—related, not equated—it with that contrast between the Celtic and the Saxon heritage, and indeed between contemporary Celts and Saxons, about which she felt so strongly. For myself I find that part of her argument thoughtful, stimulating and well worth pondering, though I am just not sure how far I can accept it.

That there is profound truth in that central, germinal "Imagination" of the two Englands I have no doubt at all. No doubt, but much anxiety. Has the second really remained—not only in Steiner's time, but still, now, in our own—"comparatively uninjured" by the first? It would seem they are not all that insulated, and that the one penetrates and contaminates the other. Perhaps the Soul of England was not seriously injured by the empirical philosophy, whose rise in England owed so much to the Scientific Revolution. But materialism has by no means been confined to philosophy, and it is significant that the history of nineteenth-century science reveals how, in regard for instance to Darwinism, there are more examples of reservation and scepticism to be found among the scientists themselves than among the protagonists of the humanities. It was much the same with Marxism, and the same again with Freudianism. It was the duty, one might have expected it to be the instinct, of literature and philosophy to bring the newcomer into the light of their own rich spiritual heritage, and then to consider in unhurried appraisal (a) how far his claims were true, (b) how far they were really new (see, for instance, L. L. Whyte's little book *The Unconscious before Freud*) and (c) whither they would be likely to lead humanity. Instead they scrambled to fall flat before the brand-new idols, and lap up every notion that fell from them, concerned only to make use of it for their own usually shallow intellectual adventures.

But the grounds for anxiety go far beyond the supine mentality of England's intelligentsia. To many people, including many English people, the England of today appears to be sinking deeper and deeper into a slough of apathy and decadence. And the question that inevitably arises in their minds is: Is the distemper terminal? There are reasons enough for supposing that it is. Against them there is only to be set the sort of desperate hope I myself cherish that, somewhere, in those subliminal depths that will only surface in response to crisis, the fundamental energy of spirit is still there. After all, strange things did happen as recently as 1940. Is the Soul of England dead already, or is it, like Jairus's daughter, only sleeping? Has the passion for equality quite destroyed the love of freedom or has it not? Such, normally fruitless, speculations as this must have been among the notions that led Faulkner Jones to write her book, based in almost equal measure on her own experience and reflections on the one hand, and on the other on what she felt can be learned from Rudolf Steiner.

Drawing on the latter she was no doubt encouraged by the reflection that the epoch of the Spiritual Soul, in which England and the English-speaking peoples are destined to play the predominant role, is still less than one-third expired. From the same source she drew the conviction that the struggle for survival of the Soul of England is significant, not for England alone, but for the world as a whole—just as (we have since seen) in 1940 the struggle for survival of the body of England was significant for the world as a whole. The contrast between the two Englands, exterior and interior, body and soul, was illuminated for her by the triune psychology she expounds at the outset. It taught her that the will is founded in the bodily nature, and that the way from the spirit to the body lies through the soul. "The will of England is paralysed because the Soul of England is asleep." But in this epoch the will and the soul mean, and mean increasingly, the self-determined wills and souls of individual men and women. It is these souls that need to be awakened if the struggle for survival is to succeed, and it is for each of these wills to do what lies to hand for it. Faulkner Jones willed to contribute her mite towards a possible awakening, and what lay to her hand was the writing of a book about English literature.

A book about English literature it certainly is, though the title, and indeed the chapter-titles, might suggest otherwise. Take for instance Chapter II "The Perceiving of Earth":

> An instinctive feeling of the need to connect Nature with Man, to bridge the gap between them, permeates English poetry . . . English people are not always aware how peculiar to themselves this attitude to Nature really is, even now, in the twentieth century: it was still less understood at the beginning of the

nineteenth century, when verses such as Byron's description of the storm on Lake Leman struck a responsive chord in the hearts of continental readers, while Wordsworth's poetry was felt as flat and uninspired.

These twin themes lead easily into comparisons between particular French, German and English poems; the characteristic *form* of English poetry, and the difficulty non-English readers find in grasping it; into quotations from Milton, Wordsworth, Shelley, Keats, Matthew Arnold, and thence in turn to a penetrating analysis of the special quality of the English language (again in contrast with French and German); and from there to such matters as the balance between thought-rhythm, phrase-rhythm and metric-rhythm and the correspondingly different effects of rhyme and blank verse—tellingly illustrated, the last, by a warm critical appraisal of the lilt in Collins's *Ode to Evening*. And it is just because of this down-to-earth, or down-to-detail treatment of which Miss Jones shows herself so thoroughly capable, that we are the more ready to follow her into the last two chapters, when she passes, by way of King Lear, from the realm of literature to the realm of myth and, always in the light of Rudolf Steiner's findings and her understanding of them, interprets in depth the legends of King Arthur and the Holy Grail.

But it is not for me to travel faster than sound and steal the author's thunder in advance. My hope is that, when the reader has heard it directly in her own voice, he will feel with me that we could do with many more such books on many more subjects.

INTRODUCTION

Note on Major C. H. Douglas (pp. 201–2)

The economic theory of C. H. Douglas ("Social Credit") was
first advanced immediately after World War I, when his book
Economic Democracy appeared. It continued to attract attention
during the '20's when A. R. Orage made it a principal platform of
his weekly periodical *The New Age*. The "flaw in the working of
the existing financial system"—namely the spurious *permanence*
of monetary capital—to which Douglas draws attention in
Economic Democracy and Steiner in his *World Economy*, and which
threatens to render unworkable a system based on free enterprise
and capital, has not been remedied, but "Douglas Social Credit"
has largely dropped out of sight. This is probably because of the
assumption which permeates his writings, though it is not crucial
for his theory, namely, that the advance of technology has solved,
or could solve, if only the financial flaw was rectified, all problems
of mere production. It was the common assumption in the days
before such "counter-productive" problems as soil-erosion, soil-
exhaustion, pollution, had begun to raise their heads.

Owen Barfield

October 1981   South Darenth, Kent

CHAPTER I

THE THREE-FOLD SOUL

FEW people in England have any knowledge of the life-work of the late Rudolf Steiner ; the fact that his teaching is at once philosophic and esoteric presents a serious difficulty to the English, who by nature are more interested in the outer world of concrete fact than in esoteric development, and who do not readily grasp the importance of conceptual thought in its relation to daily life. More than any other nation, the English are accustomed to the Baconian method of thought, and habitually reason from multiplied particular instances to the general concept : but Steiner's teaching is mainly in direct conceptual form, or in bare statements of what he claims to be esoteric fact. He always declared that those who would take the trouble to think these out and make investigations would discover, in the exoteric world, ample proof of their truth, and repeatedly pressed his hearers to regard the statements given by him as so many hypotheses, to be held in the mind and measured by facts which are available to all. He purposely avoided giving detailed illustrations from contemporary life or from history, as he considered these should be brought forward by the student himself, being the only kind of independent corroboration possible to the normal man or woman of to-day.

No one can deny the logic of such an attitude, but it makes Steiner's work peculiarly baffling to English readers, since this strikes them at first as a mixture of startling statements unsupported by evidence, and thoughts interesting in themselves, but resting on no tangible foundation of fact.

A further difficulty lies in the form in which this teaching is presented. It was given out orally, in the form of lectures, during the course of twenty-five years, from 1899 to a few months before his death in March, 1925 ; and though the actual words of the speaker were taken down verbatim, the lecture form is difficult for new readers, involving as it does considerable repetition, and implying preceding knowledge which was there in the minds of the original hearers but does not necessarily exist in the minds of present-day inquirers. Moreover, in Steiner's writings there is no effort to convince by argument, or by any direct appeal to the feelings ; statements which, if grasped in all their bearings, must be recognised as momentous, fraught with meaning for modern life, are often made in so bald, unemotional a manner that their full significance fails to strike the reader.

But the greatest difficulty of all is that Steiner's teaching, considered in its entirety, amounts to a complete revaluation of the conceptual bases of life ; it demands in the student a willingness—almost a desire—at least to consider the possibility of a re-orientation of his thought and a redirecting of his feelings : and this at the bidding of a man who died, comparatively unknown, ten years ago.

It would be idle to deny, then, the difficulty of an approach to Steiner's work : but it would be equally idle to deny that the thought-foundations and the thought-habits which we have inherited from the past are too weak to bear the weight of our tragic, blood-stained century. The outstanding feature of post-war life is the way in which facts, definite concrete events, have grown beyond the compass of human thought, and beyond the control of the human will. For instance, there has never been a time in the history of man when individual human beings have so ardently and consciously desired peace : yet the world is bristling with armaments, and militaristic passions are stirring in the breasts of men, each of whom would nevertheless receive with genuine indignation the suggestion that he personally was anxious to plunge the world into blood. Against the wishes, against the reason, against the moral judgment, of the vast majority of the individuals composing it, the world is drifting, like a rudderless ship, towards the abyss. Such a phenomenon is unique in human annals ; as unique as this other phenomenon—that, in a world made up of men and women who would be horrified at the suggestion that they should destroy food under the eyes of a starving beggar, wholesale destruction of crops and animals is permitted to go on, side by side with the slow, gradual death by inanition of millions of our fellow-creatures.

What is wrong with our thought ? What is causing this ghastly paralysis of our will ? Towards what fate are we journeying day by day ?

Those who have sufficient imagination to realise the spiritual death which seems threatening present-day humanity, should be willing to pay some attention to the work of a man who has long been regarded by many thoughtful people as the bearer of entirely new concepts, by means of which we can not only grasp what is happening around us but can arm our will to fight the evils of our age. To cure desperate diseases, only bold remedies will avail. In the brief space of a century man's physical horizon has become commensurate with earth itself, and beyond : why should we assume that the horizon of his soul and spirit is fixed and limited ? In accepting Protestantism, England accepted a drastic revaluation of Christian doctrine. Why should she refuse to consider a further evolution of the Divine Word ?

It is well to bear in mind that Christianity was, for several centuries, regarded as the creed of slaves and illiterate or semi-educated men : the fact that cultivated Romans continued so long to ignore it, is no argument against its truth. Modern science had to struggle for many years before it became accepted as a serious rival to the humanities. Indeed, it would be true to say that all vital new thought has to make its way into life in the teeth of strong opposition from those whose minds are most imbued with the old thought which is doomed to be superseded. Thus the fact that Rudolf Steiner received little or no recognition from the leading scientists, philosophers and Churchmen of his day is no argument either for or against his greatness, and should deter no earnest seeker for truth from making a critical and impartial examination of his work.

The aim of the following studies is limited and comparatively simple : the writer has taken from Steiner's work certain definite ideas and has sought to illustrate them, to give them a richer perceptual content, by showing how they fit in with facts well-known to English people. The last two chapters are based on ideas which have arisen out of a study of Steiner's interpretation of Christianity ; the remaining five are concerned almost entirely with one particular Concept or Idea : that of the Spiritual Soul ; and in dealing with this Concept the writer has limited herself mainly to its expression in and through English literature, referring in some detail to certain out-standing works, which are representative of the whole and familiar to all English people. Readers will thus be able to judge for themselves whether, within this limited sphere, Steiner's thought can throw new light on the problems of modern life.

For the sake of those who are quite unacquainted with Steiner's teaching, it is necessary to give a very brief—and therefore shallow and incomplete—explanation of two other sister-concepts : those of the Sentient Soul and the Intellectual Soul.

Steiner puts forward the hypothesis of re-incarnation, and postulates seven great periods of evolution, each lasting about 2,500 years, and extending between the destruction of ancient Atlantis and a second catastrophic event which still lies far ahead in time. In each of these periods some specific human quality is developed : those that concern this book are the Sentient Soul, developed in the Third Epoch, which covered, roughly, the period in which Egypt and Chaldea were at the height of their power : the Intellectual Soul, developed in the Graeco-Roman period—the Fourth Epoch—and the Spiritual Soul, now being developed in our own Fifth Epoch, which began in the fifteenth century and will last for at least another thousand years.

A man at the Sentient Soul stage acts primarily from motives rising out of the feeling-life ungoverned by reason. His feelings are strong and vigorous, easily stirred by what meets them in the outer world, responsive to sound, light and colour, easily fanned into passion of every kind. The whole story of Esther, in the Old Testament, is an excellent picture of the Sentient Soul in its decadence. Ahasuerus condemns the Jews to death to please Haman ; Esther is stirred into action mainly by the picture of her adoptive father sitting in sackcloth and ashes ; she risks her life by venturing into the King's sight unbidden—everything depends on the shade of feeling which stirs his soul when he beholds her. When Esther has brought about the desired revulsion in the King's feeling, the fate to which Ahasuerus condemns the Jews' enemies seems, by modern standards, as undeserved as the destruction planned by Haman for the Jews.

Mankind has long since passed this stage of evolution, but Steiner points out that every individual in youth does pass through a development which may be regarded as a recapitulation, at a higher level in some respects, of the Sentient Soul Epoch. The adolescent is swayed by feeling far more than by reason : his feelings are warm, glowing, easily stirred to passion. By the age of twenty-one, in modern man, the Sentient Soul has passed out of the embryonic stage ; and when the man is twenty-eight, the principle is fully mature in him. During these years the second principle, the Intellectual Soul, is already stirring within him, but it is not free to begin its full development till he reaches the age of twenty-eight, and does not become completely mature until his thirty-fifth year.

Two European nations, Spain and Italy, have as their special task the recapitulation, in a way suitable for our era, of the Sentient Soul evolution. The art of these countries enables us to form an idea of the Sentient Soul. In "Romeo and Juliet" Shakespeare has given us, out of Italian sources, the apotheosis of adolescent beauty. Dante, Raphael, Michael Angelo, have made it possible for us to realise to what sublime heights the feeling-life of man can rise. The more sombre glory of Spanish art, the whole life of the Spanish peasant before it was touched by modern civilisation, help to fill in the picture. Chateaubriand, writing at the beginning of the last century, said of the Spaniards :

"On ne remarque chez cette nation aucun de ces airs serviles, aucun de ces tours de phrase qui annoncent l'abjection des pensées et la dégradation de l'âme. La langue du grand seigneur et du paysan est la même ; le salut, le même ; les compliments, les habitudes, les usages, sont les mêmes. Autant la confiance et la génerosité de ce peuple envers les étrangers sont sans bornes, autant sa vengeance est terrible quand on le trahit.

"Il a peu de ce qu'on appelle esprit ; mais les passions exaltées lui tiennent lieu de cette lumière qui vient de la finesse et de l'abondance des idées. Un Espagnol qui passe le jour sans parler, qui n'a rien vu, qui ne se soucie de rien voir, qui n'a rien lu, rien étudié, rien comparé, trouvera dans la grandeur de ses résolutions les réssources nécessaires au moment de l'adversité."

The passage points the imagination to what was, in the Third Epoch, the glory of man : he was less conscious of his humanity, but more aware of the Divine, and through his feeling was capable of experiencing directly the Spiritual Powers which sustained him.

The history of Spain and Italy give us some conception of the shadow side of the Sentient Soul—the dark passions behind the Inquisition ; the disunion, the bloodshed, the treachery that disfigure the annals of the Italian City-States, even at their greatest ; the long period of sloth and decadence that preceded the Risorgimento.

When man reached the next stage of his development—called by Steiner that of the Intellectual Soul —he began to reason on his emotions ; for, though he still felt with great intensity, his intellect began the mighty task of ordering, controlling, pruning the feeling-life. While the modern man is recapitulating this stage of evolution—which he begins to do from about the age of twenty-eight, he is drawn to introspection, to self-analysis, to the discussion of those social problems which concern specially the subjective, personal life—questions of sex and marriage, for example. The full greatness of the Intellectual Soul can only be felt through the art and philosophy of ancient Greece, or through mediaeval Christian art and the highly-wrought intellectualism of men such as Thomas Aquinas. But an easier approach for the modern mind is through the art of France, the country which, according to Steiner, is the special bearer of the Intellectual Soul in our Fifth Epoch. One might

8

well characterise French literature as an elaborate analysis of every passion, every shade of feeling, that could possibly stir the human breast. Like a surgeon with his knife, stern yet merciful, the great French writer stands over the human being : no quiver of the feeling-life is hid from him, no subterfuge can divert his keen eyes from every dark corner of the heart. There is no finer school for self-comprehension than the literature of France : from Phèdre to La Cousine Bette and Emma Bovary, from Alceste to Julien Sorel—every man and woman owes it to himself and herself to make at least once this pilgrimage of mind and soul.

The shadow-side of the Intellectual Soul is to be found in an undue, a morbid, preoccupation with the subjective life ; a tendency to remain fixed at the stage of introspection ; to be too little interested in the objective world ; to overestimate the importance of the personal life ; to pry so long into dark recesses of the soul that the healthy, life-renewing breezes of the outer world are forgotten, and an unwholesome. unconquerable cynicism pervades the whole being.

The development of the third principle, the Spiritual Soul, is, according to Steiner, the special task of the Fifth Epoch. It embodies a new element, which entered the world for the first time somewhere about the middle of the fifteenth century, though in England it had been foreshadowed as early as 1215, the date of Magna Carta. England was, Steiner says, the cradle of the Spiritual Soul at its inception, and to this day remains its purest representative, though the faculty is unfolding itself gradually, to a greater or less degree, all over the globe. In other countries, either earlier-developed faculties remain strongly marked, or future faculties are already dimly foreshadowed, so that the workings of the Spiritual Soul, though they may easily be traced, are nevertheless obscured and often the result of imitation rather than of a natural, spontaneous development.

It is thus possible, from a study of English art and English history, to gain a very clear idea of the Spiritual Soul and, conversely, the concept of the Spiritual Soul, as given by Steiner, illuminates much that is obscure even to the English themselves and, rightly used, could become a key by which much that is enigmatical about England and her ways could become clear to our continental neighbours.

In the Spiritual Soul (which may be considered as free to begin its full development when he reaches the age of thirty-four) man becomes, for the first time, fully conscious of his spiritual being, his Ego. Thinking now becomes his own individual activity, for he no longer feels the thought-world as external to himself, but as the creation of his own brain. Moreover, he begins to permeate his feelings with thought, so that his soul is no longer an organ for feeling alone : in proportion as he succeeds in spiritualising his soul by thought he can contol his passions easily and naturally from within, ceasing to need so much support from external laws and conventions. He becomes able to see himself objectively, in his relationship to other men and women—a very great advance in the moral sphere, since all truly moral actions must arise from a recognition of the relation of man to man.

The Spiritual Soul finds expression in and through the physical body, into which man has completely descended for the first time ·in the course of his evolution. Because of this descent into the physical body, man has become able to make full use of his sense-organs, and thus to become aware of all that surrounds him on the material plane. This "awareness" is indeed the foundation on which the Spiritual Soul culture is built, and its most striking manifestation is the rapid development, in the last few centuries, of the physical Sciences, and the industrial civilisation arising out of them. It is universally acknowledged that modern Science and Technical Industry were first developed in England, and this country is still more completely industrialised than any other.

Closely connected with man's descent to the physical plane, and his development of the individual reason, is the growth of that world-outlook known as materialism, which denies, more or less categorically, the possibility of man's gaining direct knowledge of any sphere other than that vouchsafed to his sense organs. Isolated in his physical body, dazzled by the new earth-knowledge, overwhelmed by delight in his new intellectual faculties, the modern man tends naturally to over-estimate, not only the importance of the material plane, but also the strength and independence of his own Ego.

Two important, and apparently contradictory, ideas frequently recur in Rudolf Steiner's work. On the one hand he regarded England, the representative of the Spiritual Soul, as the true source of that materialism which has spread like a blight over Europe and is now attacking the East with great power. And, on the other hand, he admitted that the English people themselves have somehow escaped the worst consequences of the materialism they have generated. They have poisoned others, while themselves remaining comparatively uninjured.

Steiner himself did not trace fully the hidden connection between these apparently contradictory statements, for he had little exoteric knowledge of this country. He had a profound knowledge of, and feeling for, the culture of Central Europe—in a very real sense he was a representative of the true German Spirit, regarding his own work as, in many respects, a continuation and an expansion of that spiritual stream which had flowed through the great German mystics, through Goethe, through Hegel, through Wagner. But it would be true to say that, compared with his knowledge of German life, art and thought, his direct knowledge of the English language, of English literature and of English life, was very limited. He had, however, a clear idea of all that is implied by the term Spiritual Soul, and thus he actually possessed what might be termed a conceptual knowledge of this country, which should, if correct, prove complementary to our own self-knowledge and tally with the concrete facts of our history and cultural development. The German people are, according to Steiner, the representatives of the pure Ego, their highest gifts being the power of self-generated thought-activity and a certain "inwardness" which gives them a special genius for acquiring true esoteric knowledge.

The two-fold statement of Steiner, referred to above, should be considered very seriously by English people, for it emphasises the fact that, while the world has eagerly imitated and developed further the technical science and industrialised town-life of this country, yet it has never penetrated to the true sources of England's spiritual life. Indeed, the general opinion prevails that English people have no spiritual life, and no art, worth considering, and little true intellectual power, being governed by a kind of animal instinct which serves them in good stead from a materialistic point of view. This very unflattering opinion is held far more widely than is generally supposed among non-English people, and lies at the core of a certain hostility and resentment which English people tend to arouse in those belonging to other nations.

Considerable external homage, and much genuine appreciation, have been for more than a century bestowed on Shakespeare, and there are periods when current English literature has a certain vogue on the Continent ; but, nevertheless, it is no exaggeration to say that what is greatest in our literature remains to this day unrecognised by the outside world—neither felt nor understood even by those who have a good knowledge of our language.

English people themselves have always been profoundly aware of their noble literature, which has flowed in an unbroken stream from Chaucer onwards and which, with a proud indifference to continental opinion, they have felt to be, considered in its entirety, perhaps the greatest tribute that any nation has paid to the Spiritual Being of Man. They have drunk deep from its healing waters, knowing that so long as these waters continued to flow, England would never deny the Spirit. But it is nothing short of tragic that the rest of the world should assimilate the materialistic and utilitarian elements in English life, while misunderstanding and rejecting its loftiest spirituality. A still graver danger lies in the fact that the rapid changes of modern life are tending to cut us off from our own past : we ourselves are beginning to allow our spiritual heritage to slip out of our grasp, and if the present trend of evolution continues, there will soon arise in England a generation to whom the works of her noblest writers will be sealed books.

We stand at the parting of the ways, faced by the choice of a path that climbs steeply upwards, or one that descends equally steeply into the abyss of spiritual decadence—that pleasant, comfortable amble along the level, so dear to the Englishman's heart, is a psychological impossibility at this juncture. As a nation, we must go up or down ; we must make a mighty leap forward, or slip rapidly backwards. Since, according to Rudolf Steiner, we are in a special sense the bearer of humanity's Present, the guardian of the Spiritual Soul, on us rests a responsibility greater than that resting on any other national group.

An attempt to examine certain aspects of our literature in the light of new concepts may not, at first sight, appear to have much relevance to so sweeping a statement ; but a beginning must be made at some point, and these studies, though necessarily limited in scope and tentative in their conclusions, may perhaps serve to awaken interest in people whose experience, knowledge and technical skill would enable them to make important use of these and other concepts, which are available to all who will take the trouble to approach Steiner's work in the right spirit and examine it carefully in all its bearings.

*   *   *   *   *

The Ego, flashing up in its true form, for the first time in the Spiritual Soul, becomes conscious of its environment. It observes what is around it, having the power to recognise truth in the external world if it can adopt an attitude of reverence to that which is outside itself. Devotion and Temperance—which we might call a sense of proportion—are the virtues which Steiner specially associates with the Spiritual Soul, and which are, to some extent, natural to this stage of development. It is not difficult to perceive how greatly an awakening Ego would need these particular virtues ; and nowhere do they shine out more clearly than in our literature.

The most striking characteristic of our writers is a loving awareness of the external world, whether it be the world of other human beings or the material universe itself ; their art springs from devotion to what is outside themselves, and only reveals itself fully to those who are able to give up, for the time being, all feeling of Self, allowing heart and mind to flow out into the external world.

But at the source of this devotion lies self-recognition—the separation of the naked Self from the psychological ties that bind man to nature, to family, to race, even to the spiritual world itself. Man sees himself, for the first time, in the raw, stripped of everything that has been lent to him by nature and by God. The consummation of a Shakespearian tragedy is always a supreme act of self-recognition, forced on the hero by the inexorable drive of external events ; and it is in keeping with the whole concept of the Spiritual Soul that its greatest dramatist should work on a foundation of historical reality, since it is just the terrible shock of contact with the material world, the necessity for grappling, alone and unaided, with its evils, that brings man face to face with his true self. Having recognised himself for what he is, man knows there is for him only one path—the path of selfless devotion. The Spiritual Soul proceeds from Self-recognition to Self-sacrifice ; she stays not to contemplate the Ego she has discovered, but lets it pour forth in devotion to that external world which it is her mission not only to perceive, but to redeem.

It is important to recognise that this mood of soul, in its two-fold nature, has been, up to the present, peculiarly English : it is not really understood in other countries.

The German, absorbed in thought and not very aware of the objective world, continually seeks the Being of Man, but often fails to reach the point of recognising his own limited, individual Self ; although, more than any other European, he grasps the general concept of the universal human Ego.

The Frenchman is interested in all manifestations of human feeling and tends to generalise what he observes in the various individualities around him. Molière's dramatic method is the exact antithesis of Shakespeare's. The plot of a Molière play is an elaborate machinery created by the dramatist in order to bring into manifestation the archetype which he has grasped, and built up in thought, out of his observation of innumerable traits of character revealed in various separate persons living in the sense-world. His Miser, for example, represents a synthesis of all traits exhibited by all misers. No one separate miser would normally manifest them all, for the circumstances of his life would not allow him to do so ; but it would be difficult to suggest any aspect of avarice which is not embodied in "L'Avare." Such a figure belongs primarily to the Ideal world of Thought, which Steiner describes as the Etheric Plane, where it lives with intense vitality, possessed of full reality— the reality of the Intellectual Soul. But it has not the reality of the Spiritual Soul, even though one such individual as L'Avare may have lived on earth : for Steiner explains that persons who are, in a certain sense, prototypes of a whole class of people, do actually come into physical incarnation and can be recognised by the Intellectual Soul.

Molière begins from an Ideal figure, and his dramatic labour consists in a letting-down of this Ideal content into the world of external reality : hence the importance of his brilliantly constructed plots, created specially to reveal the Prototype in as many aspects as possible. But Shakespeare starts from the material world and the external personality. He does not invent his plot, but skilfully arranges the already existing material, which, especially in the case of his tragedies, has been created by the actual earth-activities of his characters themselves. His aim is deliberately to strip the personality of all its wrappings, until he lays bare the essential essence of the man—that which is purely individual, that which distinguishes him from every other human being.

The literature of Germany and of the Latin countries, by revealing and emphasising those qualities which are common to all humanity, leads the individual, in a certain sense, to identify himself with the whole race, and thus enhances his idea of himself. These literatures bring about an expansion of the inner consciousness; for the reader feels, as part of his subjective experience, not his individual Ego, but rather the potentiality of the sum-total of all the Ego-beings who make up humanity. Such an experience is most exhilarating, and fills the reader unconsciously with a sense of his own value and importance, as a member of the race.

Dante, describing in his "Divine Comedy" the mystic path of the soul, gives the loftiest possible expression to experiences through which every human being is destined to pass; those who read Dante become conscious of a heightening and deepening of their own soul life. On a less exalted plane the same is true of Cervantes. Every man in his secret heart is Don Quixote; to read Cervantes is to laugh and weep at one's own illusions and aspirations—it is a kind of purging of the soul, through self-pity, self-mockery and self-admiration. In reading the great French classics, we delight in the exercise of our intelligence ; the feelings clarify and define themselves ; all our personal experiences spring to life and fall into orderly patterns ; we enjoy our own sagacity, for the psychological motives which the author lays bare are within ourselves and we have already recognised them also in our friends and neighbours. Self-enlightenment, self-purgation through revelation of the strength and weakness of the human heart—this is what a Frenchman unconsciously expects from a work of art.

In Goethe, the Ego experiences itself in a still more intense form ; the *Faust* sprang directly from the Ego-experience of Goethe himself and to read it in the true sense is to take part in the initiation of the Ego into the spiritual worlds.

It is no wonder that, at first, continental readers find our literature tame and flat, for it presents not that which is common to the race, or to large groups of persons, but separate, isolated individualities and their quite distinctive personal experiences. Shakespeare presents individualities so great that they do actually represent the race, and as such they strike a responsive chord in the hearts of all readers, whatever their nationality ; but a study of continental Shakespearian criticism shows that, even in Shakespeare, much that gives the greatest delight to his own countrymen passes unnoticed in other lands.

Generally speaking, so far from enhancing a man's sense of his own importance and his own sagacity, English literature tends to waken him from his grandiose dream of the potentialities of the human race, into a prosaic realisation of how very little he, as an individual, has succeeded in making his own. Instead of quickening and nourishing his subjective feeling of his Ego—a very different thing from the *objective recognition* of what it is—English literature demands in the reader a complete suppression of the Self; he must sink himself into external nature, or into the Self of another man or woman, and in doing so he becomes aware of his own weakness, his own inadequacy. It is easier, for example, for a woman to dwell on the weaknesses of a Cousine Bette, or the sorrows of Eugénie Grandet, than to have to recognise how very much superior Anne Eliot is to herself. There is some strong power in the greatest English writers which makes their characters so intensely individual that a reader can no more identify himself with them than he could with a man sitting opposite to him in a train. The reader must be quick and mobile of soul, highly perceptive, possessing something of the great actor's gift of living into one part after another. It is not without significance that Shakespeare, himself an actor, has given us in "Hamlet" a picture of the Player entering so deeply into the woes of Hecuba that even his physical body is affected :

". . . all his visage wann'd
Tears in his eyes, distraction in's aspect,
A broken voice . . . and all for nothing !
For Hecuba ! "

That this descent from the ideal splendour of human passion and human power, as manifested in representative type-characters, into the narrow limits of the separate individual man, is felt as a kind of anti-climax by continental readers, accounts for much in their attitude to English literature. It helps us to understand why Byron should have been so enthusiastically admired in Europe, while his great contemporaries, Wordsworth, Coleridge, Keats and Shelley, remained comparatively unknown. Byron's rhetorical verse, springing from sheer egoism and full of his own tempestuous passions, fed the self-feeling of his readers ; every youth could imagine himself Manfred, or Don Juan, or the nobler Childe Harold, just as he could fancy himself Werther or Hernani. Byron was popular because his work was *not* character-istic of the Spiritual Soul culture.

Another peculiarity of English culture lies in the fact that it is based on the interpenetration of feeling and thought, whereas the culture of the other great European countries is marked by a distinct tendency to keep thought and feeling more separate. English philosophy cannot compare in power and range with that of Central Europe ; we have no figure equal, for sheer intellectual greatness, to Pascal ; and our litera-ture, as a whole, lacks the concentrated splendour of analytical power and the passionate intensity of feeling that distinguishes the great French writers. We have neither "grands philosophes" nor "grandes passionnées," either in real life or in art. But the culture of England ought not to be judged primarily by the range of its thought or the intensity of its feeling : its greatness lies in the extent to which, in it, thought has penetrated and "informed" the feeling-life : nowhere in the world are the feelings and actions of the masses of the people so controlled, so governed by intelligence, as they are in this country. This is the root and source of our power in the external world.

In England, Thought and Feeling are wedded ; each quite definitely acts as a check on the other and each, to a considerable extent, frustrates the other's highest possibilities. But, on the other hand, the children of this union are none other than the Spiritual Soul herself and the individualised Ego. What must be felt and recognised in our literature is not intellectual brilliance, not the apotheosis of human passions, but the manifold, subtle expression of that new element on earth—human individuality.

In the light of these concepts it is interesting to consider, first in a more general way, and later in more detail, the English writer's attitude to the material world. Like the scientist, he works primarily from sense observation, and like the scientist he builds up his feeling for the material universe from a detailed knowledge of the separate parts which make up the whole. Tennyson says of Arthur Hallam : "He brought an eye for all he saw." Wordsworth, describing his daffodils, says : "I gazed and gazed . . ." and speaking of the song of his Highland Reaper :

> "O listen ! for the Vale profound
> Is overflowing with the sound."

The English poet rarely uses the word "nature ;" but he observes with remarkable accuracy each flower, each bird, each tree, till a kind of tender intimacy grows up between them and him. He has that rare faculty of feeling the peculiar quality of an individual flower or of a whole landscape. If the ancient Greek beheld trees and flowers and streams ensouled, the English poet has allowed his own soul-life to play round them, clothing them, as in a garment, with his humanity. No flowers, no birds, have ever been loved in so intimate, so personal a way as those of our English fields and lanes and gardens. From Chaucer onwards our poets have delighted in enumerating the flowers they love, going over them one by one. We speak, whimsically enough, of Chaucer's Daisy, of Wordsworth's Daisy —his Lesser Celandine, his Cuckoo, his Green Linnet : implying far more than the mere name of a poem. Hardy wrote some tender verses, not to Shelley, but to Shelley's skylark. Tennyson, wandering in the garden of the home his family is shortly to leave, regrets the individual plants.

One of the most important thoughts in Rudolf Steiner's "Philosophy of Spiritual Activity" is that an object should not be considered a whole in itself ; it is only the percept : to complete its reality we must have in our minds its full history in time and space. A manifest impossibility ! But the more we can enlarge our knowledge of, and feeling for, the object, the nearer are we to attaining that far-off goal of its full reality.

We gain a more living feeling for this thought through art ; and the quiet meditative devotion of the Spiritual Soul, springing as it does from a union of sense-observation and creative imagination, can, by playing round an object, add immeasurably to its true content. A perfect example of this is Keats's "Ode to a Grecian Urn." The poet seems to re-create the artist's work, enfolding its beauty in the tender light of his imagination ; yet leaving undis-possessed the soul of its original creator. He may well say :

> "Thou still unravish'd bride of quietness,
> Thou foster-child of silence and slow time . . ."

For the Spiritual Soul, in its highest manifestations, does not seize with violence what is external to it : it has a delicate reverence for the truth of the outer world, remaining in humility on the threshold of the Holy of Holies. A tender warmth, enfolding yet never violating what the poet beholds in love—this is the peculiar quality of Keats's verse, with its marble firmness of outline. In this lies his spiritual kinship with Spenser, who unites with the same quality of reverent tenderness a breadth and splendour of imaginative power rare on earth. Where, in the world of art, could one find a purer sublimation of the sense-world, a more complete union of the physical and the spiritual, than his "Epithalamion" ? Less-exalted, but each well-nigh faultless in its kind, are Tennyson's "Shell" and Francis Thompson's "To a Snowflake" ; the latter, more charged with "will" than with "feeling," is a marvellous expression of the spirit in the crystal, reached from without by sheer intensity of observation.

"What heart could have thought you ?
  Past our devisal
  (O filigree petal !)
Fashioned so purely,
Fragilely, surely,
From what Paradisal
Imageless metal,
Too costly for cost ?
Who hammered you, wrought you—
From argentine vapour ?—
God was my shaper.
Passing surmisal,
He hammered, He wrought me,
From curled silver vapour,
To lust of His mind :—
Thou could'st not have thought me !
So purely, so palely,
Tinily, surely,
Mightily, fraily,
Insculpted and embossed,
With His Hammer of wind,
And His Graver of frost."

Not only the individual object, but whole land-
scapes, can be enfolded by the human personality ;
as, for example, in Spenser's "Prothalamion," in
Milton's "L'Allegro" and "Il Penseroso," where the
landscape is the very "body" in which the poet
incarnates the mood of his soul ; in Matthew Arnold's
"Scholar Gypsy"—most intimate of all expressions
of love for one special earth.

Of all the English poets, Wordsworth is most deeply
connected with the material earth, which throughout
his life was the reflecting medium for his consciousness.
Lessing reached the concept of reincarnation by logical
reasoning ; but Wordsworth reached the concept of

a pre-natal life by noting the subtle changes that occurred in his relationship to that landscape with which from childhood he had been familiar.

> "There was a time when meadow, grove and stream,
>   The earth, and every common sight,
>   To me did seem
> Apparelled in celestial light,
> The glory and the freshness of a dream.
> It is not now as it hath been of yore :
>   Turn wheresoe'er I may,
>   By night or day,
> The things which I have seen I now can see no more."

This Ode is great with the majesty of a love powerful enough to spiritualise a landscape, raising it out of its material existence into the very life of the soul. To so passionate, so selfless a lover, the earth revealed a mystery of heaven.

> "Our birth is but a sleep and a forgetting :
>   The Soul that rises with us, our life's Star,
>   Hath had elsewhere its setting,
>   And cometh from afar :
>   Not in entire forgetfulness,
>   And not in utter nakedness,
>   But trailing clouds of glory do we come
>   From God, who is our home."

A delicate attuning of his soul to the external environment is the most characteristic quality of Wordsworth, revealed with special clarity in the Ode referred to above, in "Tintern Abbey" and in "Peele Castle." The poet looks at a picture of Peele Castle in a storm, painted by his friend Sir George Beaumont. There rises up in his mind a counter-picture of the castle as he had seen it years ago. But since that time his beloved brother has died, and he realises that because of this event and its effect on his soul, his whole relationship to that particular landscape has altered. The "Tintern Abbey" poem is still more remarkable. He is revisiting a certain definite spot on the river Wye, near Tintern Abbey, after an absence of five years—as he carefully explains in the lengthy title—and the poem records a subtle change in his relationship to the landscape ; a change which makes him aware that his whole attitude to nature has altered, because of a deepening in his soul-life. Speaking of his earlier visit, he says :

> "These beauteous forms
> Through a long absence, have not been to me
> As is a landscape to a blind man's eye :
> But oft, in lonely rooms, and 'mid the din
> Of towns and cities, I have owed to them,
> In hours of weariness, sensations sweet,
> Felt in the blood, and felt along the heart ;
> And passing even into my purer mind
> With tranquil restoration . . .
> . . . Nor less, I trust,
> To them I may have owed another gift,
> Of aspect more sublime ; that blessed mood,
> In which the affections gently lead us on—
> Until, the breath of this corporeal frame
> And even the motion of our human blood
> Almost suspended, we are laid asleep
> In body, and become a living soul :
> While with an eye made quiet by the power
> Of harmony, and the deep power of joy,
> We see into the life of things.

> . . . .

> "How oft, in spirit, have I turned to thee,
> O sylvan Wye ! thou wanderer through the woods,
> How often has my spirit turned to thee !"

Describing further his relationship to nature in those early years (he was then twenty-three) he says :

> "I cannot paint
> What then I was.   The sounding cataract
> Haunted me like a passion : the tall rock,
> The mountain, and the deep and gloomy wood,
> Their colours and their forms, were then to me
> An appetite . . ."

The first part of the poem is perhaps the most perfect expression in English literature of the Sentient Soul, as the modern man experiences it.

Now, on his second visit, at the age of twenty-eight, he is aware that his soul has separated herself from this passionate embracing of nature. The Ego within him has grown stronger ; he stands facing the power with which he had formerly been intermingled. He feels this separation as a pain, but yet an advance ; for now, gathered within himself, he recognises in feeling the Spirit behind nature. He has progressed from the Sentient Soul stage to that of the Intellectual Soul, for he is now aware of a universal divine principle permeating the material universe. This feeling for what is universal—whether it be in humanity or in nature—is the special characteristic of the Intellectual Soul.

> "And I have felt
> A presence that disturbs me with the joy
> Of elevated thoughts ; a sense sublime
> Of something far more deeply interfused,
> Whose dwelling is the light of setting suns,
> And the round ocean and the living air,
> And the blue sky, and in the mind of man :
> A motion and a spirit, that impels
> All thinking things, all objects of all thought
> And rolls through all things."

But from the thirty-fifth year—though, in English people especially, its workings are felt more obscurely from a much earlier age—a new principle begins to interpenetrate the Sentient and Intellectual Souls. The maturing Ego descends completely into the physical body, and with this descent the man's attitude to nature suffers an inevitable change : he is no longer aware of the Divine behind nature, but sees her as "matter," as something that he loves, not with rapture, but with a hidden sympathy and a secret pity, since he too, with his mortal body, is part of her and shares in her death. The poetry most character-istic of Wordsworth is the poetry of the Spiritual Soul, a poetry which expresses man's redeeming love for the material earth, in all her separate, individual manifestations.

Rudolf Steiner tells us that the Sentient Soul, pouring through the astral body, prepares it for the reception of Spirit-Self ; that the Intellectual Soul, working in the etheric body shadows forth Life-Spirit ; but that the Spiritual Soul, expressing itself as it does in the physical body, is a faint foreshadowing of Spirit-Man, who will spiritualise matter com-pletely, through the power of love. And so, in a dim, far-off way, the Spiritual Soul is beginning this mighty task, whenever she turns in love to the material universe. It is fitting that "this earth, this realm, this England," should have been so deeply beloved. Rupert Brooke spoke of his body as

"A dust whom England bore, shaped, made aware,
Gave, once, her flowers to love, her ways to roam . . ."

29

The disembodied idea of one's country may at any moment become dangerous, going to the head like wine ; but love of country rooted in the soil can harm no man ; rather it ennobles him. "Britain" and "The British Empire," for example, are, perhaps not mere concepts, but certainly far less full realities than "England" or "Scotland" or "Wales" or "Canada." Similarly most of the nationalisms—and all the internationalisms—from which the world is suffering to-day, are of the conceptual order ; they are not true realities. No great art has come of them, or can come.

This personal attitude to material things is just as evident in the work of English prose-writers. Any good anthology of Essays yields ample proof. Even Lord Bacon's stiff and stately Garden—described so meticulously that he mentions by name almost every plant he would wish to be set in it—gathers "body" as we become familiar with it and captures the imagination by the very stark realism which the author's personality has bestowed on it and which makes it somewhat arid on a first perusal.

Truth of detail and the power to evoke the essential quality of an object or a scene, we find in a high degree of perfection in the work of the great French prose-writers ; in Madame de Sevigné, for instance, or in Flaubert. But the peculiar quality of the English writers is their power not only to call up the images of the external world, but to invest them with personality —with their own particular shade of feeling. Charles Lamb does this with exquisite grace.

The descriptions in "The Compleat Angler" are saturated with the personality of Izaak Walton. Once you have read the book "perceptively" you can never dissociate the man from his river, or the river from the man. Ugliness has been felt as tenderly as beauty : the ugliness of London, for instance. The opening of "Bleak House" could only have been written by one who could savour a London fog, enjoy it for its own sake ! And what pure delight there is in the description of Peggotty's boat-house, reeking of fish, on the dreary Yarmouth flats.

Balzac thought of his novels as "La Comédie Humaine" : their essential unity has no real connection with locality, but with the types of people who inhabit certain places. The place itself is interesting only in so far as it has the tendency to foster certain type-forms of human passions and instincts. Zola based his novels on the interworking of heredity and environment—again a principle universal in its application and interest.

But it is characteristic of the great English novelists that their work is local in tone and colouring. They love to "sublimate" a country or a town—witness the faithful pilgrims, proof against all laughter— who solemnly wander in search of Dickens's London or Hardy's Wessex. Many a lover of Jane Austen has visited Lyme Regis for no other reason than to enjoy the subtle pleasure of walking round Louisa's Cobb. Trollope's Barset, with Barchester Cathedral and Mrs. Proudie at its heart, is as real a county as any on the map. And who does not know Castlewood, with its rooks and its great expanse of sky ?

The importance of this appeal to feeling for places and things cannot be over-estimated, for man needs to love the material earth and the material earth needs to be loved by man. In this Fifth Epoch, man is being driven, by the course of evolution, into closer and closer contact with matter : it is essential that he should not approach matter only through the intellect, only through scientific thought. Through his own purified soul-forces, the English writer awakens loving interest in the outer world, transmuting into something higher the materialism that is right and natural for the Ego at the present stage of its development.

The soul of man is that part of his being which brings him into fellowship with others. It is just because they have the power to enshrine their profound thought in feeling that our greatest writers can be read with delight by children, young people, and those who are comparatively little developed on the side of pure intellect. Many simple folk begin by loving Dickens or Scott or the Brontës in childhood or youth, and go on reading the precious volumes over and over again, with steadily growing affection, to the very end of their lives, entering slowly into deeper and deeper strata of meaning. Men of powerful intellect and wide experience find in them unfailing springs of refreshment for the soul. Disraeli confessed to having read "Pride and Prejudice" seventeen times : and a distinguished living philosopher, now an aged man, loves to tell how he discovered Jane Austen in early manhood, and has ever since travelled round and round her six books, in happy spirals, never ceasing to draw delight from them. Deep significance lies in the fact that

Shakespeare can be read with genuine appreciation by adolescents, and even children, of all classes of society. There is nothing equivalent to this in the culture of any other country. Shakespeare, more than any other poet, has that supreme gift of himself creating the forces of mind and soul required for the understanding of his work.

All this—and infinitely more—is implied in Rudolf Steiner's statement that the Spiritual Soul is the normal medium of expression for the Ego in this epoch.

CHAPTER II

THE PERCEIVING OF EARTH

THE most important point to notice in the English poet's attitude to Nature, is that he adds to Nature something emanating from his own Individuality. Starting from the material universe, he does not pierce through the material to the spiritual—he works "forward," so to speak, to a new spirituality.

He *adds*

> "the light that never was on sea or land,
>   The consecration and the poet's dream."

And, a greater gift still, he adds to Nature something that springs from the suffering and striving of Man. The closing lines of Wordsworth's "Immortality Ode" are of very deep significance :—

> "The clouds that gather round the setting sun
> Do take a sober colouring from an eye
> That hath kept watch o'er man's mortality.
> Another race hath been, and other palms are won.
> Thanks to the human heart by which we live,
> Thanks to its tenderness, its joys, and fears,
> To me the meanest flower that blows can give
> Thoughts that do often lie too deep for tears."

This is something new in human culture : something bound up with the whole task of the Spiritual Soul. Compare with the last four lines the following sentence from "The Philosophy of Spiritual Activity" (Page 22) :—

"We can find Nature outside of us, only if we have first learnt to know her within us. The Natural within us must be our guide to her." Wordsworth actually lived this truth, which he learnt through the

34

power of Love, not through Thought.   An instinctive
feeling of the need to connect Nature with Man,
to bridge the gap between them, permeates English
poetry.   Man must not take refuge in Nature ; he
must not even be inspired by her, in the original sense
of the term ; he must be active, not passive, in his
attitude to her.

English people are not always aware how peculiar
to themselves this attitude to Nature really is, even
now, in the twentieth century : it was still less understood at the beginning of the nineteenth century,
when verses such as Byron's description of the storm
on Lake Leman struck a responsive chord in the hearts
of continental readers, while Wordsworth's poetry
was felt as flat and uninspired.   What a German, or
a Frenchman, or an Italian, expects to find in Nature-
poetry is the note of ecstasy ; something that makes
him feel the sublimity of Nature, her infinite depths,
her power, her spirituality.   The thought of Man as
a being more powerful than Nature came to de Vigny
as a new inspiration, which he made the subject of
his poem "La Bouteille à la Mer."   But this thought
is implicit in the whole of English literature ; it is so
natural to an Englishman that he never really brings
it into his consciousness, and thus fails to understand
what quality it is that continental readers find lacking
in poetry which he himself recognises as very great.
We can realise better the special quality of English
Nature-poetry when we feel how it contrasts with
that of France and Germany.

Very characteristic of French poetry is the mood of
ecstasy, the sense of being caught up and merged into

the sublime, the majestic, in Nature ; of being filled
with rapture before the Divine Presence in Nature.
From such a mood of soul sprang these lines of Victor
Hugo :

EXTASE.

"J'étais seul près des flots, par une nuit d'étoiles,
Pas un nuage aux cieux, sur les mers pas de voiles.
Mes yeux plongeaient plus loin que le monde réel,
Et les bois et les monts et toute la nature
Semblaient interroger dans un confus murmure
Les flots des mers, les feux du ciel.

"Et les étoiles d'or, légions infinies,
A voix haute, à voix basse, avec mille harmonies
Disaient en inclinant leurs couronnes de feu,
Et les flots bleus que rien ne gouverne et n'arrête.
Disaient en recourbant l'écume de leur crête,
C'est le Seigneur, le Seigneur Dieu.

Graver, more sombre, filled with a more measured
intensity of feeling are these characteristic lines of
Leconte de Lisle :

"Viens ! le soleil te parle en paroles sublimes ;
Dans sa flamme implacable absorbe-toi sans fin ;
Et retourne à pas lents vers les cités infimes,
Le coeur trempé sept fois dans le néant divin."

The poet feels Nature as a power which can purify
and heal Man.

To the German poet, the beauty of Nature seems
to bring an exaltation of the whole feeling-life, such
as Faust expresses, for instance, in the lines :

(1) "Doch ist es jedem eingeboren,
Dass sein Gefühl hinauf und vorwärts dringt,
Wenn über uns, im blauen Raum verloren,
Ihr schmetternd Lied die Lerche singt ;" . . .

In "Faust" Nature has power to heal Man. The magnificent opening of Part II describes how Faust, broken in mind and body through his own guilt and remorse, is restored through the ministrations of Nature-beings.

(2) "Kleiner Elfen Geistergrösse
Eilet, wo sie helfen kann ;
Ob er heilig? ob er böse?
Jammert sie der Unglücksmann."

The beneficent healing of his spirit is completed by the Sun-rise.

(3) "Horchet ! horcht dem Sturm der Horen !
Tönend wird für Geistesohren
Schon der neue Tag geboren,
Felsentore knarren rasselnd,
Phöbus Räder rollen prasselnd,
Welch Getöse bringt das Licht !"

It is the Divine Spirit behind Nature that is perceived and felt by Goethe. Contrast with this Coleridge's "Ancient Mariner." He too is guilty, but he finds himself abandoned to appalling solitude.

---

(1) "And yet the yearning Nature places
In every breast, upwards and onwards springs.
When high o'erhead, lost in the azure spaces,
His quivering song the sky-lark sings.
(*Latham's translation.*)

(2) "Elves great-souled though small of stature
Haste to help where help they can.
Good or evil be his nature
Pity they the luckless man."
(*Latham's translation.*)

(3) "Hark ! The Hours in storm are winging,
And, to spirit ears loud-ringing,
Now the new-born day is springing.
Rocky portals clang asunder,
Phoebus' wheels roll forth in thunder,
What a tumult brings the light !
(*Latham's translation.*)

37

> "Alone, alone, all, all alone,
> Alone on a wide, wide sea !
> And never a saint took pity on
> My soul in agony."

Nature is powerless to heal him, until from the depth of his heart he can first give to *her* his blessing !

> "Beyond the shadow of the ship,
> I watch'd the water-snakes :
> They moved in tracks of shining white,
> And when they rear'd, the elfish light
> Fell off in hoary flakes.

> "Within the shadow of the ship
> I watch'd their rich attire :
> Blue, glossy green, and velvet black,
> They coil'd and swam ; and every track
> Was a flash of golden fire.

> "O happy living things ! no tongue
> Their beauty might declare :
> A spring of love gush'd from my heart,
> And I bless'd them unaware :
> Sure my kind saint took pity on me,
> And I bless'd them unaware.

> ' 'The self-same moment I could pray . . ."

Wordsworth's flower can only give him thoughts, because something flows from the poet's heart to the flower. Man—guilty, suffering, dying in utter loneliness in the midst of Nature—must yet love and bless Nature, who of herself is powerless to help him, who must needs slay him. This is indeed a thought that lies too deep for tears ; it is a secret that the Spiritual Soul knows instinctively. For this she has sacrificed ecstasy, the sense of the Divine Presence—for the power not only to perceive, but also to love and to bless the material universe.

Wordsworth seems to have lived out in his own life this part of the mission of the Spiritual Soul—those long, apparently barren, years of his old age were part of his sacrifice. "Tintern Abbey" records the change in his Nature-consciousness that occurred between his twenty-third and his twenty-ninth years. At the age of twenty-eight he still is "Nature's priest" —he still perceives the Divine behind Nature, though it awakens in him not ecstasy, but a feeling that "subdues" him "with the joy of elevated thought." The first four stanzas of the "Immortality Ode" were written in 1802, when Wordsworth was thirty-two ; but the poem was not finally completed until his thirty-sixth year.

The Ode is thus one of the most important of human documents, for in it is revealed the transition from the Sentient and Intellectual Soul stages to that of the Spiritual Soul—a change experienced in full consciousness ; recognised as something painful, tragic ; yet accepted with noble resignation and complete understanding of all that it implies. The man knows in every fibre of his being that the spirit behind Nature has withdrawn, leaving him face to face with what Rudolf Steiner has called "the corpse" of Nature ; and he feels that nothing more can come to this dead Nature, except what Man gives to her through love and suffering. His heart accepts the task of the Spiritual Soul, which, according to the teaching of Rudolf Steiner, can only find fulfilment in the immeasurably far-off times of Spirit-Man.

"What though the radiance which was once so bright
    Be now for ever taken from my sight,
    Though nothing can bring back the hour
    Of splendour in the grass, of glory in the flower ;
    We will grieve not, rather find
    Strength in what remains behind ;
    In the primal sympathy
    Which having been must ever be ;
    In the soothing thoughts that spring
    Out of human suffering . . ."

To the thirty-sixth year of his life belongs "Peele Castle," which also reveals the transition from the Intellectual Soul stage to that of the Spiritual Soul, but to which special significance attaches because, through it, we learn that this change of consciousness has been "precipitated," so to speak, by the death of his beloved brother John, who was drowned in February, 1805. Through his experience of human death he feels all the more intensely the death, for him, of what was living in Nature. But the note of grave, high courage rings out again.

"The feeling of my loss will ne'er be old ;
    This, which I know, I speak with mind serene."

If Wordsworth had written nothing more than these three poems—and lived through the experiences they describe and imply—he would stand revealed as one of those great representative Individualities whose mission it is to endure, in an intense form, experiences characteristic of a whole epoch. But he has done more than this. In a letter of Keats, written to his friend Reynolds, there is a remarkable passage about Wordsworth which shows that the young poet—he was only in his twenty-third year—had not only a delicate feeling for the true significance of his great contemporary, but had himself experienced consciously the transition from adolescence to the first "mode" of Soul-life ; and, like Wordsworth, was fully aware—though for him it was still as a direct experience, in the future—of the tragedy of the Spiritual Soul and her divine mission.

' "Well, I compare human life to a large mansion of many apartments, two of which I can only describe, the doors of the rest being as yet shut upon me. The first we step into we call the Infant, or Thoughtless Chamber, in which we remain as long as we do not think. We remain there a long while, and notwithstanding the doors of the second chamber remain wide open, showing a bright appearance, we care not to hasten to it, but are at length imperceptibly impelled by the awakening of the thinking principle within us. We no sooner get into the second chamber, which I shall call the Chamber of Maiden-thought, than we become intoxicated with the light and the atmosphere. We see nothing but pleasant wonders, and think of delaying there for ever in delight. However, among the effects this breathing is father of, is that tremendous one of sharpening one's vision into the heart and nature of man, of convincing one's nerves that the world is full of misery and heartbreak, pain, sickness, and oppression ; whereby this Chamber of Maiden-thought becomes gradually darkened, and at the same time, on all sides of it, many doors are set open—but all dark—all leading to dark passages. We see not the balance of good and evil ; we are in a mist ; we are in that state, we feel the 'Burden of the Mystery.' To this point was Wordsworth come, as far as I can conceive, when he wrote 'Tintern Abbey,' and it seems to me that his genius is explorative of those dark passages. Now if we live, and go on thinking, we too shall explore them. He is a genius, and superior to us, in so far as he can, more than we, make discoveries and shed a light on them."

Faust, too, attains to the knowledge that man must devote himself to the redemption of the material earth—he is saved through this discovery. But he only reaches at the end of a long and, externally, destructive life, the point which Wordsworth reached naturally at the age of thirty-six ; and even so the interest of Goethe's poem lies in the saving of Faust's soul, not in the redeeming of Nature. Feeling is older, more mature, than Thought, and the Spiritual Soul can give to Man knowledge for which the Ego alone has to strive through long years.

It must be remembered that, according to Steiner, Goethe's consciousness *after* his twenty-first year, was no longer the normal one for his day. After referring to a very serious illness, which occurred when Goethe was a student at Leipzig, in 1769, Steiner says : "What happened to Goethe when he lay ill at Leipzig ? There took place what we may call a complete loosening of the etheric body, in which the life-force of the soul had until then been active ; this was so loosened that after his illness Goethe no longer had the firm connection between the etheric body and the physical body which he had before."

Wordsworth's changes of consciousness took place in the *reverse* direction, in time, to that of Goethe's. From a study of his biography one is justified in drawing the inference that when he was a child his etheric body was very much more loosely connected with his physical body than is the case with normal children ; and it was not until some point of time between his twenty-ninth and his thirty-fifth year that he attained the consciousness of the ordinary man of to-day—that of the physical body. He himself was fully aware of the importance of his "Immortality Ode," and he told his nephew, in connection with the poem, of the intensely spiritual feeling he had as a child—"I was often unable to think of external things as having existence, and I communed with all that I saw as something not apart from, but inherent in, my own immaterial nature. Many times, going to school, I have grasped a wall or tree, to recall myself from this abyss of idealism to reality." He explains to his nephew that he did not mean, in the poem, "to give a literal account of the affections and moral being of childhood ; I record my own feelings at that time, my absolute spirituality, my all-soulness."

Compare with these explanations of Wordsworth the following passage from a lecture-course given by Steiner at the Goetheanum, at Christmas, 1922. Describing the men of the third (Sentient-Soul) Post-Atlantean Epoch, he says : "And we may truly say, in the ancient wisdom of mankind there was no contrast between Nature and the Spirit. . . . Likewise they felt no contrast between Man and surrounding Nature. . . . Man recognised an inherent kinship when he looked outward to the world of bodies, and inward to the human body. He did not feel Nature as another ; he felt himself a unity—a living organism —with the remaining world."

The present writer feels justified in considering that what Wordsworth gives us is the direct experience— recorded with an accuracy of observation worthy of Science itself—of how the human being *feels* the gradual sinking of the etheric body into the physical. It is essentially an experience connected with the Soul, and Wordsworth is most careful to use the word "feel," whenever he refers to it. He learnt in *feeling* the difference between the Sentient Soul, the Intellectual Soul, and the Spiritual Soul. He reached in full consciousness the stage of the Spiritual Soul, by passing consciously through the two earlier stages. The "reflecting medium" for his consciousness, all the time, was his external natural environment, and he only became aware of these changes through noting the effects of this environment on his feeling-life. Wordsworth is thus, in a very special sense, a representative of the Spiritual Soul. He is specially able to understand how the normal man of this epoch can direct his feeling-life towards Nature ; and Anthroposophists will recognise a close connection between the Wordsworthian attitude to Nature and that aspect of Steiner's teaching which is expressed in the lectures entitled "Anthroposophy and the Human Heart," given in Vienna, in 1923.

Goethe's experience of Nature was more spiritual than that of Wordsworth ; but there was in it less of human love and tenderness. Moreover, Wordsworth's consciousness, in his maturity, is that of the present day, and, for the vast majority of mankind, that of the next two or three centuries. Goethe's consciousness is that of the more distant future, even for the "advance-guard" of the human race. It is thus important to realise that Wordsworth and Goethe, in so far as their attitude to Nature is concerned, are complementary figures ; although the range of

Goethe's work is so much vaster than that of Words-worth's, the fact still remains that there is something important in Wordsworth's poetry which can be found nowhere else in literature—something that sheds a very special light on the relationship between Man and Nature in the Spiritual Soul Epoch.

Matthew Arnold links together these two great Individualities in some interesting and suggestive verses addressed to the memory of the French writer Etienne Pivert de Senancourt, author of a now forgotten book, "Obermann"—a writer whose work Arnold, in a note to the poem, described as undeservedly neglected, and distinguished by "profound inwardness," "austere sincerity" and "a delicate feeling for Nature."

> Yet of the spirits who have reign'd
> In this our troubled day,
> I know but two, who have attain'd
> Save thee, to see their way.
>
> By England's lakes, in grey old age,
> His quiet home one keeps ;
> And one, the strong, much toiling sage,
> In German Weimar sleeps.
>
> But Wordsworth's eyes avert their ken
> From half of human fate ;
> And Goethe's course few sons of men
> May think to emulate."

Goethe conceives Nature as containing healing force for man, because his gaze pierces through the material earth to the spiritual beings who sustain and nourish it : he ignores matter itself. But to Words-worth's mature consciousness, after he has begun to unfold the Spiritual Soul, Nature is simply the material earth, and he conceives Man as redeeming her through fellowship in suffering, through human pity and love.

There is exactly the same idea, expressed with greater clarity, in ideal form, in Shelley's "Prometheus Unbound." Shelley distinguishes very clearly between Nature—the material earth—and the Spirit of Earth, a glorious Being who guides the Planet in its course through the heavens. Nature sickens and pines, while Man is bound ; she pities her son Prometheus, she suffers with him, but is quite powerless to redeem herself or to help him. She cannot even comprehend the greatness of his Spirit—she can only wait for his deliverance, knowing that he alone will have power to purify and re-create her defiled and decaying elements.

The full greatness of this conception of man's connection with Nature can only be felt out of a knowledge of Steiner's esoteric teaching : that the Spiritual Soul, finding its expression in the physical body, is closely bound up with man's task of redeeming the material earth by transforming his own body into pure Spirit, so that he becomes not man, but Spirit-man.

The English poet is more concerned with Nature herself, than with the effect which Nature produces on his own heart ; one might almost say he is seeking to feel something that is common to himself and Nature. He tries to draw her, as far as he can, into the orbit of his own human personality, to enfold her in his own feeling-life. He is most attracted by those individual manifestations of Nature which man feels to be closely connected with his daily life. Wordsworth's "To a Skylark" is a perfect example of this poetry of the Spiritual Soul.

> "Ethereal minstrel ! pilgrim of the sky !
> Dost thou despise the earth where cares abound ?
> Or, while the wings aspire, are heart and eye
> Both with thy nest upon the dewy ground ?
> Thy nest which thou canst drop into at will,
> Those quivering wings composed, that music still ! . . .
>
> To the last point of vision, and beyond
> Mount, daring warbler !—that love-prompted strain
> —'Twixt thee and thine a never-failing bond—
> Thrills not the less the bosom of the plain :
> Yet might'st thou seem, proud privilege ! to sing
> All independent of the leafy Spring.
>
> Leave to the nightingale her shady wood ;
> A privacy of glorious light is thine ;
> Whence thou dost pour upon the world a flood
> Of harmony, with instinct more divine ;
> Type of the wise who soar, but never roam ;
> True to the kindred points of Heaven and Home ! "

Shelley's "To a Skylark" is widely different in feeling, but he too seeks to create a bond between himself and the bird.

> "Teach us, sprite or bird,
> What sweet thoughts are thine . . ."

The bond between man and Nature is immanent in all the poetry of Keats, finding its most perfect expression in his "Ode to a Nightingale."

This attitude to Nature is anthropomorphic in the true, great sense which one understands more fully in meditating on the important passage in the "Philosophy of Spiritual Activity" which has been mentioned earlier : "We have, it is true, torn ourselves away from Nature, but we must none the less have carried away something of her in our own selves. This quality of Nature in us we must seek out, and then we shall discover our connection with her once more" (Page 22).

What in the bird is instinctive, must in man be raised to full Ego-consciousness ; its power of natural love, its soaring ecstasy, the objective spirituality that permeates its whole body—these are in man too, in so far as he is Earth-man, and his task is to redeem them out of Nature for his Ego. The poet of the Spiritual Soul does not merely "know" this relationship between man and Nature in the way one knows the superficial facts of life ; it is interwoven in the very structure of his physical body, in the forms of the language he speaks. He can therefore at his greatest, give expression to it in verse through which throbs not only the spirituality of his own Ego, but the power and majesty of Earth herself ; verse which bears, like the crystal, the direct imprint of the Spirits of Form.

Yet the form of English poetry presents an even greater difficulty to non-English readers than its substance, for the English poet works from a sense of rhythm entirely different from that of a German or a French poet. This difference is none the less real because it has not been generally raised into the consciousness of thought, and it very effectually cuts off the continental reader from a true appreciation of the greatest qualities of English poetry, while, on the other hand, it prevents many English people from enjoying to the full the poetry of France particularly ; the rhythm of German poetry is too strongly marked to be overlooked.

It is significant, in this connection, to notice how one great English poet speaks of another. To Spenser, Chaucer is "That Well of English undefiled." Shakespeare, referring in one of his sonnets to a rival poet, begins : "Was it the proud full sail of his great verse." . . . The young Milton says :

> "Sweetest Shakespeare, Fancy's child,
> Warbles his native wood-notes wild."

Wordsworth says of Milton :

> "Thou had'st a voice, whose sound was like the sea,
> Pure as the naked heavens, majestic, free."

Tennyson addresses Milton thus :

> "O mighty-mouthed inventor of harmonies,
> O skill'd to sing of Time or Eternity,
> God-gifted organ-voice of England."

Keats, speaking of Chapman's translation of Homer, says :

> "Yet did I never breathe his pure serene,
> Till I heard Chapman speak out loud and bold."

Matthew Arnold says of Shakespeare :

> "All pains the immortal spirit must endure,
> All weakness that impairs, all griefs that bow,
> Find their sole voice in that victorious brow."

But Tennyson, speaking of Virgil, says :

> "Though thine ocean-roll of rhythm
> Sound for ever of imperial Rome."

49

He also speaks of the "strong-wing'd hexameters of Homer"; and Gray, referring to Pindar, speaks of

> "the ample pinion,
>   That the Theban eagle bare."

The imagery is very striking; in the case of the classical poets, Homer and Pindar, the verse is felt as "wing'd," borne forward by its own rhythm. But in speaking of poets of his own race, the English poet uses most often the image "voice." The word "sail" in the Shakespearian sonnet obviously refers to the whole bearing of the ship, its manner of moving. A ship in full sail goes forward with the steady purposive motion of something moving of its own volition. The speaking voice of a human being expresses, in a peculiarly intimate way, his individuality; soul and spirit mingle to produce its delicate inflexions; it is, in a certain sense, a kind of image of the Spiritual Soul, for the Ego is felt within the Breath, which is specially connected with the astral body and the soul. Now Rhythm is an expression of the etheric body; Rudolf Steiner often speaks of the Rhythmic System in the human being as corresponding especially with the feeling-life of the heart. The Spiritual Soul expresses itself, not through the astral or etheric bodies, but through the physical body itself; and in English poetry metrical rhythm is not of primary importance —it is, of course, an essential element, but it arises out of something far more subtle, which it would be difficult to explain, to those who do not feel it naturally, without the concepts of Rudolf Steiner. The central concept of the "Philosophy of Spiritual

Activity" is that the act of thinking, of uniting concept and percept, is, in a very special sense, the conscious act of the Ego ; it is the one act in which the Ego may be said to be absolutely free. One might express the fundamental fact of our age, according to Rudolf Steiner's teaching, thus : In the midst of our feeling-life, thought begins to make its appearance. In the preceding age—which Steiner calls the age of the Intellectual Soul—thought and feeling existed more, as it were, in a state of separation. Feeling was indivi-dual, but thought flowed around the human being, forming a kind of objective world for his spiritual perception, a world towards which his feeling turned, into which he could plunge with his feeling, uniting himself to the thoughts. But now this objective thought has disappeared for man's inner perception ; it has withdrawn into the individual human beings, so that, through the "deed" of each separate Ego, it has become innumerable points of light, each point flashing up in the soul of some human being.

But just as, in the Intellectual Soul age, feeling turned outwards towards the thought world, so now feeling still turns towards the thought—towards the individual thought-power that dwells in each man's soul.

It is not, therefore, surprising that the English language should be a very subtle instrument for the expression of individual thought in such a way that it can be felt aesthetically through the form of the sentences. Rudolf Steiner explains that, in addition to the five commonly acknowledged senses, man possesses seven others—one of which is the sense of

Thought, the power of spiritual perception which enables a man to become aware of a thought which has been expressed by another person, just as, through his physical senses, he becomes aware of sound and colour.

The right way to approach English poetry is to feel, not primarily its metrical rhythm, but its thought-content, and the forms in which that content is expressed. To feel a thought is very different from thinking ; even a child, provided its soul-powers are delicate and sensitive, can feel a thought which he will only be able to grasp through the intellect years later. Moreover a thought which is so felt enters with living force into the whole being of child or man, and is in no danger whatever of becoming the "dead thought" of which Rudolf Steiner so often speaks.

English literature, more than any other, stimulates the development of this power to feel or perceive thought, which, in many English people, is already fairly acute. An Englishman does comparatively little actual thinking, as his continental neighbours are quick to notice ; but what they do not recognise so clearly is that he can receive thought objectively, by perception, with remarkable ease. For this reason it has never been necessary for the average English child to be forced through the hard, elaborate training in logical thought which has long been considered essential for the French or German boy. English educationists know this instinctively, though they would be puzzled to give a reasoned explanation of either their theory or their practice : what they do consider important is the training of the will and the feeling.

Many cultured English people still consider that if a child can be induced to browse, of his accord, among good English classics, the rest of his education may safely be left to take care of itself, in the case of a girl ; or may be regarded from a strictly utilitarian standpoint, in the case of a boy. "A comfortable doctrine, and much may be said of it."

The actual construction of any language is closely bound up, according to Steiner's teaching, with the Spirits of Form who bestowed on man his Ego. But in the case of the English language, the forms are much less fixed than those of the languages of Germany and of the Latin countries. Inflexions, for instance, have almost disappeared ; many relationships expressed grammatically in the other languages are expressed in English only through the tones of the voice ; there are remarkably few hard-and-fast rules concerning the sequence of words in a clause, or clauses in a sentence ; the language contains a very high proportion of monosyllables. As a result, English, whether spoken or written, expresses very directly the individuality of the speaker or writer ; he receives comparatively little "support" from the language itself. English can be dull, banal, inept, to an extraordinary degree, and it can be the most subtle, the most powerful, the most majestic of tongues ; everything depends on who is using it. Its high percentage of monosyllables allows a great writer an almost unlimited range of phrase-rhythms, for it must be remembered that in English there is no "stop" between the separate words as such ; three monosyllables, spoken as a phrase, may have exactly the same sound-value as a three-syllable word ; but whereas the latter must always be pronounced with one fixed accentuation, three monosyllabic words may be combined in several different ways, their whole tone and sense being altered according to which of the three bears the main accent. A careful study of Milton or Shakespeare—or indeed of any of our great poets—reveals how powerful combinations of monosyllables can become, and what great mobility they give to the language.

It seems no exaggeration to say that in English the forms of the language are "loosened," so that the Ego of the writer or speaker can penetrate very deeply into them, moulding them more directly than is possible in the Latin languages or in German. Even the phonetic values of the vowel sounds are far from fixed ; and, to a fine ear, the variations reveal much concerning the individuality of the speaker. Indeed English people are specially sensitive about their speech because they know instinctively that their speech "betrays" them. A pure vowel-sound must always be pronounced in one way, but a diphthong offers various possibilities—some people stress one element of it slightly more than the other ; there can be no ruling in such a matter—diphthongs have a way of breaking through rules, and most of the English vowel-sounds are really diphthongs.

In English literature, "form" is, then, the most important element. The true, essential rhythm of English poetry springs from its thought-forms ; the right approach to a poem is to "feel" its meaning, and to grasp in feeling also the construction of the whole, and the inner relationship of clause to clause. If the poem is thus felt, the reader will notice the beautiful rhythm which arises out of the natural pauses that occur, that are necessary for the sake of the meaning ; out of the balance of the sentences. There will also be metrical rhythm, but the beat of Iamb and Trochee will be felt as subdued, held in check, by the more subtle rhythm arising out of the thought-forms. A very strong metrical rhythm is nearly always—though there are notable exceptions—the mark of second-rate verse, in English ; much of the poetry of Scott, Byron and Longfellow has this characteristic.

When Gray refers to the poetry of Dryden, although he evidently admires it greatly, he uses an image which suggests that in this poetry metrical rhythm predominates.

> "Behold where Dryden's less presumptuous car,
>   Wide o'er the fields of glory bear
>   Two coursers of heroic race,
>   With necks in thunder clothed, and long-resounding pace."

The rhythmical gallop of Dryden's stirring verse is typical of an age in which French influence was strong in our literature ; it is magnificent rhetoric, but not great poetry. Our greatest poetry is that in which the feeling-rhythm is broken, mastered, by the thought-rhythm ; yet in such a way that it emerges from this discipline as something finer, more subtle, more spiritualised.

This is very difficult for continental readers to grasp, accustomed as they are to strong metrical rhythms, which "bear" the spirituality of the poetry and carry the reader along on a powerful stream of feeling. Needless to say, the thought-rhythm of an English poem can only be felt by those who have a very complete grasp of the language ; it vanishes entirely in translation, and, moreover, in a translation the metrical rhythm is almost inevitably exaggerated, so that it no longer bears a true relationship to the feeling of the poem, which should be as a veil of warmth within which the thought may live. The transfigured Asia in "Prometheus Unbound," might well stand for an Imagination of the greatest English poetry.

> "Child of Light ! Thy limbs are burning
> Through the veil which seems to hide them,
> As the radiant lines of morning
> Through thin clouds, ere they divide them ;
> And this atmosphere divinest
> Shrouds thee wheresoe'er thou shinest."

One of the most perfect examples of thought-rhythm is Collins's exquisite "Ode to Evening ;" the first five stanzas make one complete sentence, and all their delicate music depends on the reader's feeling the poet's meaning and giving due value, by the length of the pauses he makes, by the tones and inflexions of his voice, to the beautiful, highly-wrought structure of the whole passage. There is no rhyme and the beat of the metrical rhythm is so stilled as to be scarcely perceptible ; to emphasise it would be to destroy the poem.

> "If aught of oaten stop, or pastoral song,
> May hope, chaste Eve, to soothe thy modest ear,
> Like thy own solemn springs,
> Thy springs and dying gales ;

O nymph reserved, while now the bright-hair'd sun
Sits in yon western tent, whose cloudy skirts,
With brede ethereal wove,
O'erhang his wavy bed ;

Now air is hush'd, save where the weak-eyed bat
With short shrill shriek flits by on leathern wing,
Or where the beetle winds
His small but sullen horn,

As oft he rises, midst the twilight path,
Against the pilgrim borne in heedless hum ;
Now teach me, maid composed,
To breathe some soften'd strain,

Whose numbers, stealing through thy darkening vale,
May not unseemly with its stillness suit,
As, musing slow, I hail
Thy genial loved return."

It is well known that the construction of Shakespeare's blank verse changed materially with every year of his life. In his early plays the verse is, on the whole, regular and has a comparatively marked metrical rhythm ; rhyming endings are frequent. But year by year the line becomes more broken, the regular metrical rhythm vanishes, rhymes hardly ever occur ; and more and more the deeper, more subtle music of thought-rhythm sounds for those whose ear is attuned to perceive it.

Delightful as we may find the "Midsummer Night's Dream," there is far more powerful magic in the sheer sound of the later plays.

The following passage from "A Winter's Tale," approached from the standpoint of metrical rhythm, becomes nonsense. But if the thought is felt, if the due pauses are made, if full feeling-value is given by the voice to the succession of imperatives, then out of the form rises the true Shakespearian music.

> *Paulina* :   "Music, awake her ; strike!
> 'Tis time ; descend ; be stone no more ; approach ;
> Strike all that look upon with marvel.   Come ;
> I'll fill your grave up : stir ; nay, come away ;
> Bequeath to death your numbness, for from him
> Dear life redeems you.   You perceive she stirs ;
>   (*Hermione comes down*)
>
> Start not ; her actions shall be holy as
> You hear my spell is lawful ; do not shun her
> Until you see her die again, for then
> You kill her double.   Nay, present your hand ;
> When she was young you woo'd her ; now in age
> Is she become the suitor."

Paradoxical as it may seem, it is none the less true to say that Grammar is a sounder way of approach to English verse than Prosody ; not a cut-and-dried, intellectualised Grammar, but an aesthetic feeling, natural or acquired, for the "bones" of the language. Such a feeling is indispensable for a full appreciation of the later plays of Shakespeare, or of the harmonies of Milton's blank verse ; and, indeed, without such a feeling it is impossible for anyone to have a sense of style in English prose ; such qualities as "colour," "rhythm" and "vowel-music," important as they undoubtedly are, are yet only secondary in the prose of the greatest masters—of Swift, for instance, or of Addison or Newman. Their power springs from a complete—an almost miraculous—mastery of form.

The name "Grammar School" was given out of a deep instinctive feeling for the reality that underlies

English culture ; and there is no more beautiful instance of the working of the principle of evolution in human life than the way in which a feeling for grammatical constructions, acquired in the first instance by a conscious, prolonged, detailed study of Greek and Latin—the languages of the Fourth Epoch—became in this country the key to the artistic values of English, pre-eminently the language of the Fifth Epoch.

It would be a tragic blunder, fraught with far-reaching consequences, if the non-English peoples should fail to recognise the esoteric significance of English literature ; and it would be fatal to the whole future development of this country, if the English themselves allowed their great inheritance to slip out of their grasp. If we consider its astonishing variety, its range, its power and, above all, the extent to which, though springing from the purest aesthetic feeling, it is yet impregnated with profound thought, we can say, without fear of exaggeration, that English literature is one of the greatest achievements of the human race. It is one of the most precious gifts of the Spiritual soul, a gift that the Ego of man cannot afford to reject, containing as it does an antidote to that materialism which is the inevitable growth of our age.

The English language is already used more than any other, and is likely to spread. How much longer will it be able to stand the terrible test of diffusion ? Will it break down prematurely into dead, debased forms ? Or will it remain powerful enough to mould the spiritual life of the countless millions destined to use it as their natural speech ? A very grave responsibility rests on all those who are still in the direct sphere of influence of the English Folk-Spirit. Much depends on whether that which lay behind the inspiration of the great English writers, that which existed in their aesthetic consciousness, can be raised into the thought life of the modern man. It is useless to deny that, just as Religion needs to-day a firmer basis than pure faith, so the esoteric significance of the great art of the past must now be grasped in thought, if these works are to remain living forces in the present.

The modern man is becoming more and more conscious, less and less guided by instinct ; he cannot approach a work of art springing from the life of an earlier century and take it directly into his feeling—he must be able to interpret the spirituality of the past in the light of the spirituality proper to his own age. Plays such as "Hamlet" or "King Lear," or "Faust" mean to the modern man something they could not possibly have meant to the men of the ages in which they were written, or even to the men of the last century. The spiritual content of a true work of art has this property : that it develops and unfolds itself with the onward march of time, remaining eternally true, yet revealing new aspects of its truth to every succeeding age.

The esoteric teaching of Rudolf Steiner, received and applied in full consciousnsess, can not only take the place of that key formerly received unconsciously through the training in Greek and Latin ; it can give to our literature a fuller spiritual reality than it has ever yet had, opening up this reality to the comprehension of non-English races, and of those Englishmen whose environment and upbringing puts between them and the art of the past a barrier even greater than that of the intervening centuries. On the other hand, our literature could become one of the most important paths by which this esoteric teaching might enter into the normal daily life of men and women. Out of the living communion between the past and the present might well spring a new birth of great literature—a second Revival of Learning, rich with new forms of art, mighty with the strength of abounding life.

CHAPTER III

THE PERCEIVING OF THE EGO

THE Spiritual Soul not only becomes aware of truth in the world of nature, but she has also the power to recognise truth in other human beings—to recognise the Ego, as it appears in other men. Simultaneously with a consciousness of Self, the human being, at this stage, can become conscious of the Self of another. Not only has he gained special power to perceive by means of the five universally recognised senses, but he has also the beginnings of the development of those other senses enumerated by Rudolf Steiner—the Sense of Thought, for instance ; and—most important of all—the Sense of the Ego. He can become "aware" of the Ego of another human being, here in the physical universe. He has moreover a certain natural reverence for the Spirit as it manifests itself in another man or woman.

According to Rudolf Steiner, the outstanding characteristic of Goethe was that, though he took as the material basis of his poem the Faust legends, his work was nevertheless "original" in a far more profound sense than is generally recognised, since Goethe himself lived out in the course of his life the "Faust experience." What he unfolds in his poem is the actual evolution of his own Ego ; he was thus, in a very literal sense, the spiritual creator of his "Faust." But the very opposite is true of Shakespeare : his special power lay in the fact that he was able—through what must have been complete self-immolation—to experience in himself other human Individualities.

Rudolf Steiner tells us, for instance, that the original Danish prince, Hamlet, was a re-incarnation of the Trojan Hector, and that Shakespeare, in his play, was able to reveal the full significance of this particular incarnation of that great Individuality. We are justified in drawing the conclusion that Shakespeare was able, directly or indirectly, to establish contact in the spiritual world, with this Individuality ; and, by whatever means the contact was achieved, he must have had the power to suppress, to hold back, his own Self, and allow this lofty Ego to pour itself into him. Thus, through an act of self-abnegation, a most important incarnation of a powerful Individuality is preserved in its essential form for a world which must otherwise have remained ignorant of it, since the real Hamlet had not been able to leave abiding traces behind him.

It is given to very few people to achieve complete understanding even of those who are most beloved and nearest to them in daily life, for only the purest, most disinterested love will unlock for us the secret places of another heart and mind. How great must have been Shakespeare's power to love—how pure and delicate his soul, which could vibrate to every emotion that stirred another heart—how mighty his capacity for iron self-restraint ! Nowhere in the whole range of his works can one say with complete certainty : "Here Shakespeare is voicing his own thought ; here he is recording his own suffering." But strong, living, immortal, his characters arise— in a very real sense "heirs of his body," incarnating through him into the world of human Imagination.

Yet, nevertheless, the Ego of Shakespeare is stamped on his work as unmistakably as the Ego of Goethe is expressed in "Faust." It is to be found in the "physical body" of his plays, in their form ; in every line of his blank verse. Whether it be Lear or Caliban, Falstaff or Cordelia—however infinitely varied may be the interests, the thoughts, the feelings of his characters— they all speak with the Voice of Shakespeare. It is the sound of this Voice that has always been most precious to his own countrymen, penetrating deep through the heart into the will, stirring more profound regions of their being than could possibly be reached even by the treasures of wisdom and humanity expressed in the words themselves. The Central European approaches Shakespeare more "en philosophe," and by so doing he has undoubtedly stimulated the Englishman to bring more profound thought to bear on the plays than he otherwise would have done. But it is a mistake to imagine that Shakespeare has been neglected in England. Henry Crawford, in Jane Austen's "Mansfield Park," was nearer the truth when he remarked : "Shakespeare one gets acquainted with without knowing how. It is a part of an Englishman's constitution. His thoughts and beauties are so spread abroad that one touches them everywhere ; one is intimate with him by instinct. No man of any brain can open at a good part of his plays without falling into the flow of his meaning immediately." It is significant that Jane Austen says, "the flow of his meaning"—not "the flow of his rhythm."

Wordsworth well knew the deep-rooted connection

between Shakespeare and the Soul-life of his country-men when he wrote, in 1807 :

"We must be free or die, who speak the tongue
That Shakespeare spoke." . . . .

He was expressing, not a rhetorical sentiment, but a simple fact—overwhelming in its simplicity.

Rudolf Steiner, in a lecture entitled, "Symbolism and Phantasy in relation to the Mystery Play, 'The Soul's Probation,'" associates rhymed verse especially with the culture arising out of the recapitulation in our Epoch of the Intellectual Soul stage. Speaking of rhymed verse, he says : "The final rhyme is closely connected with the remarkable soul condition which, after man has entered the present evolution, is expressed through the culture of the Intellectual Soul, or Mind Soul. Taken fundamentally, the time in which the Intellectual Soul arose in men, in the Fourth Post-Atlantean period of civilisation, is also the time when, in poetry, the memory dawned of the experiences of the olden time, which extended into the ancient Imaginative World. This remembrance is expressed in the end-rhyme."

Alliterative verse he specially associates with that recapitulation of the Sentient Soul stage, in Northern and Central Europe, into which Christianity was first received. But speaking of our own age, he says, "Modern man . . . only knows speech as the expression of a content . . . not that which the Sentient Soul wants to introduce by the repetition of the consonant, and what the Intellectual Soul wishes to express in the closing rhyme. The Spiritual Soul

65

can really no longer use rhyme in this way ; so man must now use other means."

It is interesting to consider in the light of this last sentence, blank verse, the greatest and most character-istic of English metres, the chosen vehicle of the Elizabethan Dramatists and of Milton. Attempts to imitate it in other languages—in French, for instance —have never proved successful. It discards rhyme ; it has no fixed caesura ; it breaks through metrical rhythm ; it can bear innumerable irregularities. It seems to possess no strength, no spirituality, of its own —weak blank verse is more prosaic than the lamest prose. In what, then, lies its power ? In the fact that, more than any other known metre, it allows free expression of the individuality of the writer. Its strength is the strength of the Ego of the man who writes it ; its spirituality is his spirituality. Even a superficial study of the great writers who have used blank verse as their medium of expression reveals that each man has his own individual way of constructing it, each man gives it a certain unmistakable stamp. The greater the verse, the more strongly individual is its sound. No one with an ear for the English language could mistake the plaintive "lilt" of Fletcher for Marlowe's "mighty line"—or for the passionate intensity of his friend Beaumont—or for the curious, rich, labouring splendour of Chapman's involved sentences ; still less could anyone fail to recognise the remarkable differences in spirit, in feeling, in texture, between the blank verse of Shakespeare and that of Milton.

But it is obvious that to feel the true power of blank

verse implies a certain definite development of the "Sense of the Ego." Over and above every other artistic value in his work, the writer of blank verse expresses his own individuality—not directly, but through the way of self-abnegation. The more completely he can flow out in devotion to his subject, the more completely does his unconscious will stamp his Ego into the forms of the language he uses. The reader, on his part, must actively recognise the individuality of the writer ; must feel it deeply ; must become united with it in spirit—over and above his recognition of what has actually been created by the writer. This spiritual union between reader and writer, this "marriage of true minds," is the magic spell which takes the place of that power in the Word itself, which, Steiner tells us, gave to the ancient languages their loftiest spirituality.

Just as the Spiritual Soul has sacrificed the power to feel the Divine behind Nature, in order to perceive more clearly the "corpse" of the material universe, so too she has sacrificed something of the Divine in language—to perceive more clearly the human Ego. For what is true of blank verse is true, to a greater or less degree, of our literature as a whole ; when we speak of "style," we mean neither more nor less than this : the expression, through the form, of the writer's individuality—an elusive quality that cannot be taught or imitated, or even described, but only perceived by the Ego-sense of the reader. Needless to say, the same is true of other literatures ; but the peculiarly formless, fluid nature of the English language makes it a very perfect instrument for the expression of human individuality ; considered simply as a language, English has sacrificed more of the Divine than has German, or French, or Italian. A careful study of the way in which French critics use the word "style" shows that to them it implies something subtly different from what it means when used by English critics—something more external, more capable of analysis, more the result of *conscious* choice, or endeavour, on the part of the writer.

Although blank verse is the characteristic English metre, yet, apart from the Elizabethan Dramatists and Milton, it has been little used by our poets : nevertheless its influence has permeated even those lyrical forms which, at first sight, might appear to have nothing in common with it. Anglo-Saxon poetry was alliterative ; but perhaps the greatest of all exponents of alliterative verse in England was Chaucer's contemporary, Langland, whose work sprang from a deep understanding of the true nature of the Christ Impulse. Chaucer consciously discarded alliteration, and as regards the form of his verse passed definitely into the Intellectual Soul stage, using, though in a manner adapted to the English language, the smooth, metrical flow of line and the end-rhymes already perfected in France. In the matter and spirit of their poetry both Langland and Chaucer reveal themselves, in different ways, as men of the new Spiritual Soul Epoch ; but in its form their verse represents a recapitulation of the two earlier stages of the Sentient Soul and the Intellectual Soul. It was not till the sixteenth century that blank verse appeared at all, and the chief work of Shakespeare's immediate predecessors seems to have been the preparation of the new vehicle.

It is true to say that, after the perfecting of blank verse, rhyme, though it continued to be used with great effect, became in a subtle way different : it became of less essential importance in the verse of most poets than it is in the verse of Chaucer. In Chaucer's verse, the end-rhymes are of great importance to the feeling-tone. The very smoothness and regularity of his metres cause the voice unconsciously to accentuate the rhyme—the voice, so to speak, falls inevitably, with gentle emphasis, on the end-word, just as it does in reading French poetry. But after the sixteenth century writers of lyric poetry tend to break the metrical rhythm, to rely more on the rhythm arising from thought-forms, and thus frequently the rhyme goes almost unnoticed, as the sense flows past it, to pause, perhaps, in the middle of the next line.

It is characteristic of English rhymed verse, that the rhyme, like the metrical rhythm, is subordinated to the thought. The degree of the subordination is a measure of the relationship between, "feeling" and "thought" in the poem : it indicates in a delicate way the balance between the Soul-forces of the poet and his Ego. The Spenserian Stanza for instance, with its intricate weaving of rhymes—the rhythm hardly ever so broken that the rhyme passes without due emphasis, yet nevertheless quite definitely subdued to the thought—is in itself a symbol of the peculiar fascination of the "Faerie Queene :" that magic blending of the purest spiritual beauty, the passionless beauty of flawless gems or the starry heavens, with a rich, warm, languorous, all-pervading soul-quality that baffles analysis or description.

Equally significant is the Stanza of "In Memoriam"; the ear is strongly impressed by the inner rhyme, but the outer rhyme, by comparison, echoes only faintly, the result being a very delicate balance, a kind of rhythmic alternation of thought and feeling—which is the very essence of the poem, considered as a whole.

This harmony, in English literature, between Form and Substance is one of its most striking qualities. At its highest, the Form is the unconscious expression of the writer's own individuality: and the Substance is the manifestation of the individuality of some other Being, or of some aspect of the material universe—perceived and bodied forth through the power of selfless Devotion. Its most precious gift to Man is to lead him out of himself; to make him see and love that Earth to which he owes his humanity; to make him enter with his whole being into the experiences of others, into the very essence of other men and women.

It is instructive to consider side by side Goethe's "Wilhelm Meister" and Boswell's "Life of Johnson." Each is unique of its kind. "Wilhelm Meister" is essentially self-revelation, the story of the development of a human being seen from "within." In spite of the rich diversity and living force of the characters, one has the feeling that they are presented not primarily for their own intrinsic interest but because they are "experiences" of the hero: they are, so to speak, "projections" of Goethe himself, part of the etheric world in which that mighty Spirit is unfolding itself.

But Boswell, in spite of his naïve vanity and stupid self-conceit, was not, in a deep sense, at all interested in himself—or even conscious of himself—as an individuality. The passionate interest of his life was Samuel Johnson. Thought, feeling and will in him, were all straining towards one goal : to perceive, and to reflect back, the individuality of his friend, as it manifested itself here on earth, in one particular life. It is impossible to deny that but for Boswell the full reality of Johnson's great personality would have perished with the England in which he lived, and of which he was, more than any other one man, the representative.

Because "Wilhelm Meister" was written from the plane of the Ego, it possesses the universality of the human spirit ; it becomes, like "Faust," an Ego-experience of the reader. But the quality of Boswell's book is the polar opposite of this universality. What emerges from it is the figure of one of the most intensely individual human beings who have ever lived. No man could possibly identify himself with Samuel Johnson. Yet Boswell confidently expects his readers to enter with whole-hearted pleasure into the minutest details of his hero's personal habits— how he ate and drank, for instance, and his opinion of the dinner provided at the house of a mutual friend.

To let one's mind dwell on "Wilhelm Meister" and then on Boswell's "Life," is to gain a living percept of the distinction between the Ego manifesting in the etheric world of thought, and the Ego when it becomes individualised through sinking down into the physical body. It is significant that we have in our literature no book of the self-revelatory type worthy of comparison with "Wilhelm Meister": indeed we have no book at all like it, and no example of autobiography that can claim to rank among the greatest books in our language. But on the other hand there is nothing equivalent to Boswell's "Johnson" in French or German; and English literature is specially rich in great Biographies—books which represent years of patient, loving absorption, on the part of the writer, in the life of some other man or woman. Often the biographer is himself a famous person leading a busy external life, yet finding for years a deep spiritual joy and refreshment in thus sinking himself into another Individuality. Such Biographies have nothing in common with mere sensational prying into the details of a great man's private life, on the one hand, or with unimaginative academical research on the other.

When books of the self-revelatory type—whether they call themselves Novels or Memoirs is immaterial—begin to pour out of the English Press, it is a serious sign that all is not well with the spiritual life of the nation : for to become conscious of the individualised Ego—as distinct from the universal Ego— leads a man directly into appalling, humourless Egoism, unless he can turn his gaze outwards and forget continually that Self of which he cannot help being conscious. For a man so individualised as Johnson to begin "revealing" himself to others would be simply gross—a psychological impossibility ! An

instinctive recognition of this danger has led Englishmen to seek the spirit not within, but outside themselves.

*　　　*　　　*　　　*　　　*

In a remarkable set of lectures entitled "Evolution
in the Aspect of the Realities" Rudolf Steiner describes
the spiritual characteristic of the solid element, Earth,
as being the fact that it, and it alone, in our Universe,
is the bearer of Death.　"Earth is the element in which
Death appears, and may be experienced."　"In reality
man alone dies, for he has developed his individuality
so far that it descends into his physical body, in which,
during earth-existence, he must become real.　If we
grasp this, we must say : Man alone can truly experience Death.　Thus for man there is . . . a real
overcoming of Death."

One would be justified in inferring from this
concept that at the present stage of evolution the
more completely a man is individualised, the more
completely his Ego is expressed in the physical body,
the more fully and overwhelmingly does he experience
Death.　Since, according to Steiner's teaching, the
English have descended more deeply into the physical
body than any other race, one would expect to find, in
English literature, a very special expression of Man's
relationship to Death—more intense, more poignant,

73

more soul-shattering, than is to be found in any other language. That this does indeed exist, no one who feels the full greatness of Shakespeare's tragedies can deny. Goethe's Faust can hardly be said to "die" at all : he experiences no break in consciousness. While he is still alive, his eyes lose their power to see the things of earth and open towards the spiritual world. But "Lear" will remain for ever a Sign and Symbol for Man of his titanic wresting of his Ego-conscious-ness from Death, in the darkness of the material universe.

It may be said that the English lyric poet, as well as the Dramatist, reaches his greatest height in the contemplation of Death ; and in so far as the Spiritual Soul in the past has transcended Death, she has done so through Love, entering so deeply into the Being of another that Death itself could not utterly divide her from the object of her selfless devotion. Hence a very special interest attaches to English elegiac poetry.

> "Dear beauteous Death ! the jewel of the Just,
>   Shining nowhere but in the dark ;
> What mysteries do lie beyond thy dust,
>   Could man outlook that mark !

Tennyson's "In Memoriam" is unique in elegiac literature : there exists no other expression of grief for the dead at once so poignantly personal and so restrained, so far-reaching in its imaginative sympathy. Its very length makes it remarkable ; through nearly three thousand lines of unbroken beauty, Tennyson sustains the reader's interest in this one theme, an epic achievement, justly regarded as his master-work. The poet himself warns us against taking the poem in a heavy, dogmatic way; but although its fragmentary form defies regular analysis it has perfect artistic unity and, in the light of Rudolf Steiner's teaching, must be regarded as closely connected with the deepest spiritual history of its century, and a very striking "document" of the Spiritual Soul.

Underlying the comparative neglect of "In Memoriam" in recent years, there is this idea : "A man cannot *really* feel such living intensity of grief at the age of forty, for a college friend he lost at the age of twenty-three. Mourning the dead was a Victorian convention. Nowadays we cannot regard such a poem as sincere."

From the numerous post-war plays which have dealt in one form or another with the subject of the rapid sinking of the dead into oblivion, the general impression emerges that, however passionately a dead man or woman may have been loved, if he returned to earth some years after death his presence would create embarrassment rather than pleasure. He would find his place filled—no one would really want him. In the French play translated into English under the title of "The Unknown Soldier," this bitter thought is carried even further : not death itself, but the mere shadow of death hovering over the man is enough to cut him off from the world of the living. Such conceptions in their crudest form can arise only from the feeling that love is a kind of habit, the breaking of which can only cause pain till new habits are formed. Certainly death can have no lasting sting for the survivors when such is the case ! But the plays are by no means crude in their psychology ; they have a basis of truth, which their authors are right in putting forward for recognition. We are protected from feeling the worst horrors of death so long as our most passionate love arises directly out of the natural ties of blood or instinct, for Time and Nature so work together that with the physical body disappears also the love that was, in its essence, created by the body. Even the love that is connected more with the Soul than the body, though it is longer-lived, does not last indefinitely, for the astral body, as such, is no more immortal than is the material body.

But the love that is purely of the spirit cannot share in this merciful oblivion, and the full significance of Tennyson's suffering can only be grasped in thought through the whole concept of the Spiritual Soul, and in relation to the particular age in which he lived.

Rudolf Steiner teaches us that not until the coming of Christ to earth did it become possible for love purely spiritual, yet completely individualised, to awaken between Ego and Ego, unrelated by ties of blood or nature ; and that not until the age of the Spiritual Soul could the Ego so draw into the physical body that it might be perceived therein, and loved in its pure essence, while it trod the earth as Man. "In Memoriam" is unique as a work of art because it is directly inspired by a definite, specific instance of this highest type of human love, which, though the possibility of it exists for all, is nevertheless still so rare and precious in its flame-like purity.

It is evident that for Tennyson the tie that bound him to Hallam transcended any "natural," earthly tie : their spiritual union was so strong a reality that no question of exclusiveness could possibly arise—any earthly tie formed by either only became an added interest to each. Tennyson's own family affections were specially strong, and one of the most poignant passages in the poem is addressed to his beloved brother:

> " 'More than my brothers are to me'—
>   Let not this vex thee, noble heart !
>   I know thee, of what force thou art
> To hold the costliest love in fee—"

Indeed, there was in his love for Hallam no shadow of selfishness, nothing that could act as a bar to their natural ties of blood or marriage, or to the forming of other friendships. In the brief four years of their acquaintance, both men were part of a brilliant group of friends, all of whom had a special love and admiration for Hallam ; and to Tennyson, the culmination of his joy in his friend's love was the latter's engagement to his sister Emily. In one section of the poem, the poet tries to picture what Hallam's life would have been, had he lived to reach old age. He sees him happy as a husband, as a father ; great as a thinker ; great in service to the world. He makes no exclusive claims for himself in this life—only the joy of beholding his friend live.

> "I see myself an honour'd guest,
>   Thy partner in the flowery walk
>   Of letters, genial table-talk
> Or deep dispute, and graceful jest."

But whatever separate ties the two might form on earth, Tennyson cannot think of his own spiritual essence, except as merged in the spirit of his friend.

"Till slowly worn her earthly robe,
　　Her lavish mission richly wrought,
　　Leaving great legacies of thought,
Thy spirit should fail from off the globe ;

What time mine own might also flee,
　　As link'd with thine in love and fate,
　　And, hovering o'er the dolorous strait
To the other shore, involved in thee,

Arrive at last the blessed goal,
　　And he that died in Holy Land
　　Would reach us out the shining hand,
And take us as a single soul—"

One cannot fail to realise, through many delicate touches, that while the poet's love for Hallam was purely spiritual, springing from the Ego itself, yet for him the spiritual essence of his friend was expressed in and through the physical body. Tennyson had a very special consciousness of the physical body as the Temple of the Spirit. He felt the Eternal in man as Will, at once objective and subjective, and instinctively connected it with the earth-element :

"O living Will, that shalt endure
　　When all that seems shalt suffer shock,
　　Rise in the spiritual rock,
Flow through our deeds and make them pure."

It would be difficult to find a more powerful artistic expression of the very core of Steiner's teaching concerning the Spiritual Soul : that the Ego, at this stage, expresses itself in the physical body as Will ; and that from this penetration of the Ego into the physical springs directly the moral sense.

78

The poet dwells with a strange intensity of imaginative power on the dead body of his friend—this forsaken Abode of the Ego—moving majestically through the physical universe, on its way to burial. In the still, marble beauty of the verse, Earth becomes one with the physical body of Man—both encompassed about with love, wholly penetrated and "informed" with love.

> "Sphere all your lights around, above ;
>   Sleep, gentle heavens, before the prow ;
>   Sleep, gentle winds, as he sleeps now,
> My friend, the brother of my love. . . .
>
> Calm and deep peace on this high wold,
>   And on these dews that drench the furze,
>   And all the silvery gossamers
> That twinkle into green and gold :
>
> Calm and still light on yon great plain
>   That sweeps with all its autumn bowers,
>   And crowded farms and lessening towers,
> To mingle with the bounding main :
>
> Calm on the sea, and silver sleep,
>   And waves that sway themselves in rest,
>   And dead calm in that noble breast
> That heaves but with the heaving deep."

Because he recognised and loved the very spiritual essence of his friend, as he moved here on earth in physical incarnation, Tennyson, when that friend died, was brought face to face with death in its most absolute form—the extinction of the spirit ; for with the death of the body, there vanished for him the Ego which had dwelt in it. The intensity with which he had felt the spirit of his friend, was the measure of the intensity with which he felt the blankness, the darkness of death. Few can have suffered as Tennyson did, for to few has it been given to perceive the Ego so clearly, and to love in so purely spiritual a way, while still anchored firmly to the consciousness of the physical body. In the past, Nature stood between Man and Death ; in the future, the human being, according to the teaching of Steiner, either out of his own spiritual strength, or because he is from birth endowed with clairvoyant organs, will be able to penetrate the mystery of Death far enough, at least, to be saved from the keenest pain it can cause. But Tennyson stood at the parting of the ways ; he possessed in full measure those greatest gifts of the Spiritual Soul—the sense of the Ego and the power to love ; but he lived just at the end of the "Age of Darkness," he was chained to the physical body. Thus he was, if one may be pardoned the expression, "condemned" to love, with pitiless intensity, a spiritual being from whom he was remorselessly divided, cut off—who had vanished into the blackness of the unknown.

Emily Brontë in "Wuthering Heights," which was published in 1847, and thus was probably written during the very years when Tennyson was composing "In Memoriam," was struggling to give artistic form to the same phenomenon. Wild, immature and unsatisfying as the book is, compared with Tennyson's poem, yet it grips the mind with a certain primitive power. Its very limitations have given it a strange, controlled, unearthly intensity. The difference in tone between "Wuthering Heights," and "In Memoriam," is a measure of the difference between an Idea realised with living power in the mind, alive in the etheric world ; and an Idea brought down to earth, lived out, experienced in actual fact—and, in the earth-element itself, impregnated with the Christ.

Both works have at their core, Death ; Death breaks asunder a purely spiritual union between two persons who recognise each other as spiritual beings, here on earth, in the physical body. There is ample evidence in "Wuthering Heights," that Emily Brontë did not intend the relationship of Heathcliff and Catherine to be taken as connected with sex, in the ordinary sense of the term ; for instance, neither is deeply perturbed by the marriage of the other—it is made quite clear that both felt the bond which united them as something beside which marriage, as it is generally understood, was trivial and unimportant. Death destroyed the body of one partner in the union ; the other suffered the intolerable, unrelenting torment of being cut off from the living Spirit. This is the secret of Heathcliff's agony, as it is of Tennyson's. It explains why Tennyson dwells with such anguish on the burial of his friend's body, and the strange incident of Heathcliff's digging away the earth from Catherine's grave, when, after eighteen years of grim endurance, mind and body begin to give way under the strain.

Those who might be inclined to consider such agony as merely the result of a morbid frame of mind, show how little they realise the stark horror lying behind the words : "The Ego descends completely

81

into the physical body, and there experiences Death."
Coleridge knew better : he knew that linked with
Death is his more terrifying companion—

> "The Night-mare Life-in-Death is she,
> Who thicks man's blood with cold."

Tennyson in actual fact—Emily Brontë, not only in
imagination, but, as her poems testify, in direct
mystical experience—lived out, as individuals, what
it means to be a *conscious* prisoner of the Body, cut
off from the Spirit. They endured in consciousness
what humanity as a whole was passing through, in
varying degrees of unconsciousness, during their
lifetime—for the date of the composition of these
works is most significant. Both were written when,
according to Rudolf Steiner, humanity descended
most deeply into matter—into the death-bearing
forces of the universe.

Hallam died in Vienna, of a sudden lesion of the
brain, in September, 1833. The inner history of
Tennyson's life between that date and 1842 can only
be surmised. He retired into solitude and obscurity ;
severed himself, as far as he could, from external ties,
giving up, for several years, writing to his friends, or
receiving letters from them.

On his own confession, he was strongly tempted to
seek death, as the only possible cure for his intolerable
grief. Seventeen years after Hallam's death that
suffering was still, in essence, unabated, though
mastered and controlled by the poet's will :

> "Ay me, the sorrow deepens down,
> Whose muffled motions blindly drown
> The bases of my life in tears."

His poem, "The Two Voices," gives some clue to the deep cleft that suddenly opened up between heart and will, on the one hand, and thought on the other. In the world outside, the same abyss yawned. Humanity was enduring the final destruction of the last traces of the ancient wisdom ; Faith as an active life-principle was in full decay ; Science was already steadily undermining the foundations not only of orthodox Christianity, but of the whole social fabric.

Karl Marx had not yet come to England, but at the time of the composition of "In Memoriam," was already recognised as an important leader among advanced socialistic thinkers and had been banished from his native country. The thought behind "Das Kapital" was already in existence, and the industrialised society which gave Marx the clue to the particular form in which this thought finally crystallised, was none other than that of Tennyson's England, the England of the eighteen-forties. What exists to-day in Russia is the offspring of a union between the thought of Marx and the England created by the Industrial Revolution.

In the last months of 1833 a ship bore from Italy, on the final stages of its journey, Hallam's dead body ; at that same point of time, H.M.S. "Beagle," with the young Darwin on board (he was about a year older than Hallam) was engaged in its epoch-making five-year cruise : ships of destiny, both of them, sailing uncharted seas of the human spirit.

It was in the midst of these waves of Ahrimanic thought, beating so powerfully on the high shores of this world, that Tennyson wrestled with Death. "In

Memoriam" tells little of the struggle, much of the final victory :

> "I trust I have not wasted breath :
>   I think we are not wholly brain,
>   Magnetic mockeries ; not in vain,
> Like Paul with beasts, I fought with Death."

It is known that, through nine years of obscure solitude, the poet subjected himself to an arduous self-discipline ; overcoming by sheer force of will the paralysis of grief ; concentrating his strength on mastering the technique of his art ; working over, with ruthless self-criticism, what he had already written. He published nothing save a few isolated poems in these years, but when the 1842 volume did appear, it placed him at once among the masters of the English language. No one reading these poems— even those of special psychological interest, such as "The Two Voices"—would imagine that they had been written by a man struggling against a spiritual agony that came near to destroying him, body and soul. Considered in the light of "In Memoriam," they stand as the consummation of Will's triumph over the Soul. For in their bland, polished beauty, not only is there nothing to suggest effort, but little to suggest that the poet had quite special powers of feeling. What Tennyson did was to hold back the deepest, strongest powers of his Soul until he had wholly penetrated them with thought, and until his will had chiselled out a faultless instrument for her use. Though a few stanzas of "In Memoriam" were written soon after Hallam's death, it was not until after the poet's thirtieth year that the work of composition really began, and the poem was not completed till he was forty. It was thus composed during that period of life which Rudolf Steiner assigns especially to the development and culmination of the Spiritual Soul. The nine years of strife ended in a victory which freed the poet from the grip of Death, exactly in that year—1842—which Rudolf Steiner gives as the moment when humanity's "descent into matter" touched its lowest point ; the seven last years of its composition marked the beginning of the long upward swing into Light.

Just how this victory was won remains Tennyson's secret. But his great poem contains indications that during these years he entered, through deep, prolonged meditation on the Being of his friend, into a mystical state in which he felt again the presence of the dead man : love piercing, flame-like, the blackness of death.

In section XII, he describes how his mind concentrated itself with intense force on the image of Hallam's body, travelling homeward by sea :

> ". . . I cannot stay ;
>   I leave this mortal ark behind,
>   A weight of nerves without a mind,
> And leave the cliffs, and haste away,
>
>   O'er ocean mirrors rounded large,
>   And reach the glow of southern skies,
>   And see the sails at distant rise,
> And linger weeping on the marge,
>
> And saying : 'Comes he thus, my friend ?
>   Is this the end of all my care ?'
>   And circle moaning in the air :
> Is this the end ?   Is this the end ?

> And forward dart again, and play
>   About the prow, and back return
>   To where the body sits, and learn
> That I have been an hour away."

In a later section, he describes how, one summer night, alone in the garden of his family home, the thought of the dead man awoke in him with great power : the words of the dead came back to his memory with special force : all his love sprang up like living flame in his heart.

> "So word by word, and line by line,
>   The dead man touched me from the past,
>   And all at once it seem'd, at last,
> The living soul was flash'd on mine,
>
>   And mine in this was wound, and whirl'd
>   About empyreal heights of thought,
>   And came on that which is, and caught
> The deep pulsations of the world,
>
> Aeonian music measuring out
>   The steps of Time—the shock of Chance—
>   The blows of Death.   At length my trance
> Was cancell'd, stricken through with doubt.
>
> Vague words ! but ah, how hard to frame
>   In matter-moulded forms of speech,
>   Or even for intellect to reach
> Thro' memory, that which I became."

In section CIII, Tennyson describes a dream :

> "A vision of the dead,
>   Which left my after-morn content."

The passage is too long to quote, and a summary would destroy the delicate truthfulness of the images ;

but most students of Rudolf Steiner's teaching, reading it even apart from its context, would understand it in feeling and recognise it as the revelation of a true mystical experience. There are many other passages in the poem which suggest that the poet, through the intensity and purity of his love, did actually break through the barrier of Death, though only for brief moments, and never in such a way that the clarity of absolute knowledge became his.

Active love is much more than feeling ; it is feeling spiritualised by thought, strengthened by will. Tennyson's thought was not powerful enough to overcome the Ahrimanic thought of his day, but, allied with his great forces of Soul and Will, it sufficed to reveal the enemy for what he was, to strip him bare of subterfuge, and to awaken a new, living active faith in Christ, his mighty Opposite :

"Strong Son of God, immortal Love."

It is significant that Tennyson, bearing as he did the forces of the Spiritual Soul, should experience Christ through feeling and will, rather than directly through thought. His love, pursuing the lost spirit of his friend, led him with unerring instinct to the Raising of Lazarus, which Steiner's teaching places so near the very heart of the Mystery of Christ and the human Ego. He cannot grasp in thought its significance ; he sees it, not through Lazarus himself, but through Mary—yet through Mary his feeling does recognise dimly the connection between Lazarus and Christ, and, passing into the will, pours itself out in loving deed.

87

"Her eyes are homes of silent prayer,
　　Nor other thought her mind admits
　　But, he was dead, and there he sits,
And he that brought him back is there.

Then one deep love doth supersede
　　All other, when her ardent gaze
　　Roves from the living brother's face,
And rests upon the Life indeed.

All subtle thought, all curious fears,
　　Borne down by gladness so complete,
　　She bows, she bathes the Saviour's feet
With costly spikenard and with tears."

Tennyson's final answer to Death is Love ; but it was the result of an individual triumph of the will.　None knew better than he himself that the Enemy was still at large, unrouted, in the battlefield of the outer world.　The greatness of his victory is the measure of the man's individual strength ; but he was well aware that the fundamental problem he had to face, the separation of Knowledge from Faith, remained unsolved for mankind as a whole and, in a certain sense, for his own mind.　He could not, with pure thought, destroy the abstract intellectualism that his soul rejected as false.

"A warmth within the breast would melt
　　The freezing reason's colder part,
　　And like a man in wrath, the heart
Stood up and answer'd 'I have felt.'"

But the strength of Tennyson—and the strength of the Spiritual Soul—lies in this : he may not have power to solve the problem, but he can at least *perceive* the problem ; he is not blinded by the specious glory of intellectualism ; he is saved, through his purified heart-forces, from confusing Knowledge with Wisdom.

> "Who loves not Knowledge ?   Who shall rail
>   Against her beauty ? may she mix
>   With men and prosper !   Who shall fix
> Her pillars ? let her work prevail.
>
> But on her forehead sits a fire :
>   She sets her forward countenance
>   And leaps into the future chance,
> Submitting all things to desire.
>
> Half-grown as yet, a child, and vain,
>   She cannot fight the fear of death.
>   What is she, cut from love and faith,
> But some wild Pallas from the brain
>
> Of Demons ? fiery-hot to burst
>   All barriers in her onward race
>   For power.   Let her know her place ;
> She is the second, not the first.
>
> A higher hand must make her mild,
>   If all be not in vain ; and guide
>   Her footsteps, moving side by side
> With Wisdom, like the younger child :
>
> For she is earthly of the mind,
>   But Wisdom heavenly of the Soul . . ."

It is this clarity of vision, a clarity arising not from thought, but from feeling purified by thought and strengthened by will, that gives to the Spiritual Soul a certain fortitude, a certain power to *wait*—to hold back her forces—to refrain from clutching eagerly at some premature, false solution of the problem facing her. It gives her also the power to see Truth, when at last Truth is vouchsafed to her. Rudolf Steiner, in his lecture on the Beatitudes explains that the one which specially applies to the Spiritual Soul is the fifth : "Blessed are the pure in heart, for they shall see God."

Tennyson's final message to his age is summed up in the Prayer which forms the Introductory Verses. But the closing lines of the poem are of special interest to students of Anthroposophy, for they show how Tennyson reached dimly, through Love, what Steiner puts forward as a definite teaching : that towards the end of the nineteenth century a very marked change took place in the spiritual life of humanity. Up to this point of time—according to Steiner's teaching— the direction of evolution was, "downward," into matter : with every passing generation, the human spirit sank more deeply into the physical body. But the very lowest point of the descent was reached towards the mid-nineteenth century, and as the twentieth century dawned humanity definitely turned its face towards the Light : in every new generation, the Ego will tend to detach itself, little by little, from the physical body, ceasing to be the Prisoner. From the middle of the twentieth century onwards, a few children will be born with a certain natural power of seeing into the Spiritual worlds (a power entirely different from the atavistic "second sight" of fortune-tellers and mediums), and, as time goes on, this gift— which will be connected with a specific organ in the brain—will gradually become again the common possession of humanity.

Tennyson, as he dwells on the rare power and beauty of his friend's spirit, can only account for him by regarding him as the type and fore-runner of a new race of men, possessed of faculties undreamt of in the nineteenth century. After describing the wedding of a member of his family, his mind turns to the thought of the child that may be born of the union—and here he seems to accept the idea of a pre-natal existence :

> "A soul shall draw from out the vast
> And strike his being into bounds,
>
> And, moved thro' life of lower phase,
> Result in man, be born and think,
> And act, and love, a closer link
> Betwixt us and the coming race
>
> Of those that, eye to eye, shall look
> On knowledge ; under whose command
> Is Earth and Earth's, and in their hand
> Is Nature like an open book ;
>
> No longer half-akin to brute ;
> For all we thought and loved and did,
> And hoped, and suffered, is but seed
> Of what in them is flower and fruit ;
>
> Whereof the man, that with me trod
> This planet, was a noble type,
> Appearing ere the times were ripe,
> That friend of mine who lives in God."

The influence of "In Memoriam" on the educated classes of England, for at least ten or fifteen years after its publication, can hardly be over-estimated, and, in lessening waves, this influence continued to spread all through the rest of the century, penetrating gradually, through a thousand channels—press, pulpit and school—into the life of the nation as a whole.

Southey said, in 1823 : "Every year shows more and more how strongly Wordsworth's poetry has leavened the rising generation."

De Quincey, in 1835, said : "Up to 1820, the name of Wordsworth was trampled underfoot ; from 1820 to 1830, it was militant ; from 1830 to 1835, it has been triumphant."

Tennyson's influence was more immediate, and therefore more overwhelming, than Wordsworth's ; each of them in turn, so to speak, mounted guard over the spiritual life of England. Mackail, in his "Life of William Morris," gives an interesting quotation from some reminiscences, written many years later, by Canon Dixon, who had been an undergraduate in 1855.

"It is difficult to the present generation to understand the Tennysonian enthusiasm which then prevailed both in Oxford and the world. All reading men read poetry, poetry was the thing ; and it was felt with justice that this was due to Tennyson. Tennyson had invented a new poetry, a new poetic English ; his use of words was new, and every piece he wrote was a conquest of a new region. . . . I am told that in this generation no University man now cares for poetry. This is almost inconceivable to one who remembers Tennyson's reign and his reception in the Sheldonian in 1855."

Such reminiscences are by no means isolated, and a study of English life in the fifties and sixties of the last century will show that it is no exaggeration to say that by 1859—the date of the publication of Darwin's "Origin of Species"—the feeling-life of large and influential sections of the upper and middle classes was "leavened" by Tennyson's "In Memoriam." One is justified in saying that Tennyson's fate forced him to grapple with the materialistic thought of his day, and he conquered Death not only for himself, but for countless contemporaries. To many a man standing in agonised perplexity of mind between Rome on the one hand, and the sweeping triumphs of Darwinism on the other, this great poem must have been a clear trumpet-call through the darkness. Like Christian, they must have gathered strength and courage, as they heard the voice of Faithful, marching ahead of them through the Valley of the Shadow.

The brilliant group of Cambridge men who had regarded Hallam as their leader and a bright particular star destined to out-shine them all in glory, was now playing no small part in the national life. W. A. Thompson eventually became Master of Trinity; Trench became Archbishop of Dublin; Alford, Dean of Canterbury; Blakesley, Dean of Lincoln; Merrivale, Dean of Ely; Richard Monckton Milnes, J. M. Kemble, Stephen Spring-Rice—all these men were important leaders of thought, and it needs no great flight of imagination to realise how deeply moving to them, and to many others who had known him personally, must have been this spiritual resurrection of Arthur Hallam from the stricken heart of his friend. That men of such varied gifts were unanimous in their high opinion of Hallam is no mean testimony to the latter's power. Young as he was when he died, his fame had spread to the sister university. Mr. Gladstone, who had known him at Eton, said of him : "It would be easy to show what in the varied forms of human excellence he might, had life been granted him, have accomplished ; much more difficult to point a finger and say, 'This he could never have done.' "

CHAPTER IV

THE ROSE

THE varied activities of any nation would, on close examination, prove to be more homogeneous in character than is usually supposed. Natural Science, developed first in England on the basis of Bacon's "Novum Organum," depends on induction from data gathered by sense perception. The "material" is passive : the scientist's mind is intensely active. But Goethe's scientific method was more allied to religious meditation : his thought was more "inward," less akin to the logical intellect. He postulated, more or less consciously, a spirit within or behind Nature, which might pour itself into man if man could succeed in making himself receptive to it. By the Goethean method of thought, man first becomes receptive, while the outer world reveals to him its "spirit." It is true that the German scientists have not pursued this method, but Rudolf Steiner traces a direct line of descent for his Spiritual Science from the Goethean mode of thought, which because of its "inwardness" is homogeneous with that of the great German philosophers and musicians.

English literature, like English science, turns its gaze outwards : it is based on perception. Science uses mainly the commonly accepted sense-organs, but Steiner enumerates twelve, not five, including among them the faculty of "perceiving Thought" and "perceiving the Ego." English literature demands for its full appreciation a high development of these senses ; it also demands that the reader should

95

not approach it passively, prepared only to receive, or with purely meditative thought : he must be, simultaneously, receptive in feeling and active in thought. English literature is a great school for the exercise of individuality, as well as for the perception of it as it manifests itself in outer life.

English Science, which finds its most characteristic expression in technique, the application of scientific principles to the needs of daily life, has brought to man leisure, freedom from the dull drudgery of manual toil, the possibility of rapid movement over the earth's surface. It has immeasurably increased the bounds of his earth horizon, the richness of his objective experience.

English literature has immeasurably increased man's social horizon. The peculiarity of the greatest English authors is that their works can be read over and over again without palling on mind or heart. They grow on the reader, and eventually both author and "characters" become as living a part of his world as those who form his daily circle, bringing sweetness and light, gentleness and beauty, humour and gaiety into his life, as effectually as if they were his intimate friends : they *are* his intimate friends, dear and precious to his heart. One would not say this of the great French writers. Their books stir the heart deeply, delight and interest the mind, enlarge and clarify the understanding, add infinitely to man's conscious knowledge of human nature : but the reader can rarely regard the characters in these books as personal friends. One may feel reverence or pity or tenderness for them— but not love. Still less could one feel love for Faust.

It is necessary here to distinguish between the three types of love we know on earth.

There is the love of a higher being for a lower, an image of the divine, sacrificial love of Christ for Man. This is the love which the greatest Russian writers have striven to portray, which they have actually succeeded in portraying, though gropingly and falteringly as yet.

Then there is the love that a lower being may bear to a higher, the reflection on earth of Man's love for God, a love which finds its loftiest expression in Dante's "Divine Comedy."

But there is also the love whose essence is neither sacrifice nor worship, but an equal blending of both; which arises between two beings equal and yet different, whole and perfect in themselves, yet mutually self-supporting—the relationship between God the Father and God the Son, which is mirrored faintly on earth in the love that arises between human beings of equal, though different, strength. It is this third type of love, potentially the most perfect of the three, which gives to English literature its highest, its most spiritual beauty : this is the Rose of England, an earthly image of that Virgin-Rose beheld by Dante in the highest Heaven.

Human love is born of the material universe, when the Spirit finds itself imprisoned in its house of clay, cut off from all other living Spirits. Only the Ego which has descended fully into the physical body can know the horror of this isolation, and the intense desire of the Prisoner that some other Spirit should break through his prison walls to give him the unspeakable solace of finding himself not alone. All are equal in this solitude of the flesh : there is no higher or lower.

> "Suffolk first died : and York, all haggled over,
>   Comes to him, where in gore he lay insteep'd,
>   And takes him by the beard, kisses the gashes
>   That bloodily did yawn upon his face ;
>   And cries aloud, 'Tarry, dear cousin Suffolk !
>   My soul shall thine keep company to heaven ;
>   Tarry, sweet soul, for mine, then fly abreast,
>   As in this glorious and well-foughten field
>   We kept together in our chivalry !' "

This is the voice of human love.

Steiner teaches us that of all the Divine Beings, Christ alone has experienced death ; for He alone has had the power to descend into the material earth. It may be that He alone, of all the Divine Beings, knows how man loves his fellow-man.

The symbol of Divine Love is the Trinity : human love is the trinity of thought, feeling and will, brought into perfect balance, and flowing out into the being of another. Love between two human beings reaches its highest perfection when they are equal, though different, in power, for then is achieved that perfect equipoise born of two equal forces, mutually supporting each other in space : the image of the material earth itself. Spenser describes it thus :

> "For love is a celestial harmony
>   Of likely hearts, composed of stars' concent,
>   Which join together in sweet sympathy,
>   To work each other's joy and true content,
>   Which they have harboured since their first descent
>   Out of their heavenly bowers, where they did see
>   And know each other here beloved to be."

Gray's description of Venus suggests a being whose essence is "poise," who moves freely in space because she has achieved perfect balance.

> "Slow, melting strains their queen's approach declare :
>   Where'er she turns, the Graces homage pay ;
>   With arms sublime, that float upon the air,
>   In gliding state she wins her easy way."

Power to move freely in space comes only from a perfect balance of physical forces, whether these are in a human body, or incorporated into the principles of a machine. Human love, at its highest, gives to those who achieve it the same kind of freedom in the psychic and spiritual planes of existence that physical balance gives in the material universe. It gives spiritual and psychic "poise," and a sense of inner power akin to that which fills the athlete when he feels body and mind working in perfect harmony, or the airman when he feels his machine responding to every movement of his will.

Human love is essentially a kingly attribute : its expression is the power that is born of perfect inner control. The concept "king" implies a duality : the king exists only in virtue of his people ; together they form a two-fold reality. In the highest sense he can only reign—that is, manifest power on the earth—if he can find in his people the equal but opposite force which enables him to achieve, through them, a perfect balance. Similarly, a people achieve a sense of power in and through their king.

Tennyson felt Love as a kingly being :

"Love is and was my King and Lord,
And will be, tho' as yet I keep
Within his court on earth, and sleep
Encompass'd by his faithful guard—"

Rudolf Steiner speaks of "Two" as the number of manifestation on the material place. Human love comes into being subjectively whenever a man or woman brings thought, feeling and will into a state of balance, and directs them outwards, in devotion, but it can only become manifest in creative earth-activity when two such out-pouring forces meet and bring each other to rest, in mutual balance.

Christ Himself cannot work creatively on earth except in so far as the out-pouring of his Divine Love can be "held" and made manifest by an out-pouring force of love from man towards Him. The extent to which Christ can work with power on earth depends on the extent to which human beings can love. When the isolated individual turns in love to Christ, He can work subjectively in that man's being, but the full power of earth-love only becomes manifest from the inter-action of human beings in mutual love. When the inter-locked love-force of two or more human beings can flow out towards the Christ, then can begin not only a subjective working of Christ in the individual, but an objective manifestation of his power on earth.

"Where two or three are gathered together in My name, there am I in the midst of them."

It is a strange thought that Love and Death should have this attribute in common : each can only be brought fully into man's consciousness through the other. We live in the midst of death, but never become, in any real sense, conscious of it, except through the death of one we love. It was Tennyson, not Hallam, who experienced death. Goethe presents death from "within," from the standpoint of the person who dies : the closing scenes of Faust—his triumphant ascent into the Spiritual worlds—have no parallel in English literature. Dante also sees death as an inner experience of the human being. But Shakespeare shows death from the earth-side, from the stand-point of those who look on and behold the living Spirit vanish from their ken. Othello meets Death when he stands by the dead body of Desdemona :

"My wife ! My wife ! what wife ? I have no wife."

It is equally true to say also that we may live in love, as we live in death, without raising it fully into our consciousness. Death, in breaking asunder the balanced love-forces of two human beings, makes clear, with terrifying power, the reality of Love's two-fold nature. Death, too, wears "the likeness of a kingly crown." His power, like the power of Love, is absolute on earth. These two, and Man himself, form a trinity, in which is imaged the Divine Trinity.

Although in this fifth Post-Atlantean Epoch man, descending to the physical plane, is brought into direct, and spiritually perilous, contact with the death-bearing forces of the material universe, yet it is this very descent into matter which affords a natural basis for the unfolding of human love. For, according to the teaching of Steiner, until his Ego could express itself in the body, man could only develop his conscious, individual will to a very limited extent. He might feel love as an inner, subjective warmth ; he might achieve a lofty concept of love ; but his actual deeds of love, carried out concretely on earth, were inadequate, compared with the richness of his thought and feeling. The essence of the Spiritual Soul Epoch is that in it the Ego penetrates the feeling-life, and is provided with a natural physical basis of expression in the blood, so that man in this Epoch is helped by the natural, normal conditions of his age to develop will-power, and make it commensurate with his thought and feeling. Temperance, in its widest sense, is not only possible but natural to the human being at this stage. Rudolf Steiner speaks of Temperance and Devotion as the two basic virtues of the Spiritual Soul.

The highest type of Englishman, especially, finds it comparatively easy to achieve a certain balance between thought, feeling and will. Whether he achieves it or not, it is certainly the goal towards which he strives, consciously or unconsciously. What he most fears and distrusts is "excess" in any direction— excess of zeal, excess of feeling, undue absorption in the life of thought. Temperance is the source and secret of his sense of humour.

Hamlet's advice to the Players is a lesson in Temperance, and one feels, in reading it, that Shakespeare himself is in heart-felt agreement with the Prince :

". . . if you mouth it, as many of your players do, I had as lief the town-crier spoke my lines. Nor do not saw the air too much with your hand, thus : but use all gently : for in the very torrent, tempest, and—as I may say—whirlwind of passion, you must acquire and beget a temperance that may give it smoothness.   O ! it offends me to the very soul to hear a robustious, periwig-pated fellow tear a passion to tatters, to very rags, to split the ears of the groundlings. . . .   Be not too tame neither, but let your own discretion be your tutor : suit the action to the word, the word to the action ; with this special observance, that you o'erstep not the modesty (i.e., moderation) of nature."

This virtue of Temperance lies at the very core of Hamlet's tragedy : he himself possesses it naturally to an exceptionally high degree, but his lot is cast among those who not only do not possess it, but are unaware of its existence.   From the Ghost, with his passionate insistence on vengeance, to the fatuous Osric, all the other characters, save Horatio, lack inner control.   Well may the Prince say to Horatio :

> "Dost thou hear ?
> Since my dear soul was mistress of her choice
> And could of men distinguish, her election
> Hath seal'd thee for herself ; for thou hast been
> As one, in suffering all, that suffers nothing,
> A man that fortune's buffets and rewards
> Hast ta'en with equal thanks ; and bless'd are those
> Whose blood and judgment are so well co-mingled
> That they are not a pipe for fortune's fingers
> To sound what stop she please.   Give me that man
> That is not passion's slave, and I will wear him
> In my heart's core, ay, in my heart of hearts,
> As I do thee."

The Ghost's demand for vengeance, addressed to a man who can speak in these terms, is a tragic anachronism.

Hamlet's nature is such that he cannot bring himself to will an action which is out of harmony with what he thinks and feels. He knows that Claudius should not be allowed to live, but his mind instinctively rejects the "revenge" motive, although, in spite of all its rich endowments, it can bring forth no other. He struggles in vain, until the end of the play, to bring about that inner harmony which alone can make his action satisfying to himself. He finds no difficulty in killing Rosencrantz and Guildenstern, because he sees through their knavery and is convinced that they thoroughly deserve the fate they have courted by their foolhardy rashness in coming

> "between the pass and full-incensed points
> Of mighty opposites."

Why then can he not kill his uncle, whose guilt is deeper and more obvious than that of mere paid emissaries?

A passage in Rudolf Steiner's "Lectures on the Gospel of St. Mark" throws much light on this problem:

"I direct your attention to the figure created by Shakespeare in his Hamlet. Anyone who knows the development of Shakespeare, as far as it can be known externally, and especially one who is acquainted with it through Spiritual Science, will know that Shakespeare's Hamlet is none other than the transformed real Prince of Denmark, who once lived. I cannot now go into everything underlying the historical form of the poetical figure of Hamlet; but by means of the researches of Spiritual Science, I can show you a striking case of how a man, a spirit of the olden times, re-appears in the post-Christian age. The real figure underlying what Shakespeare represented as Hamlet, is Hector. The same soul that lived in Hamlet,

lived in Hector. . . . A personality such as that of Hector
stands before us in the pre-Christian age ; then comes the
intervention of the Mystery of Golgotha into human evolution,
and the spark is kindled in the soul which causes a figure, a
prototype of Hamlet to arise. . . . We may ask : Why did
Shakespeare express it thus ? He did not know. But one who
can investigate the connections by means of Spiritual Science,
knows that forces were at work behind these things. The poet
creates in unconsciousness, because before him stands, as it
were, first the figure which he creates, and then, as in a tableau,
of which he himself knows nothing, the whole Individuality
with which the figure is connected. Why does Shakespeare
select particular qualities in Hamlet and sharply emphasise
them, qualities which perhaps Hamlet's own contemporaries
would not have noticed ? Because he observes them in the
background of time. He feels how different a soul has become
in its transition from the old life to the new. . . .

It is perhaps not quite accurate, yet not far wrong, to say
that if we go very far back in human evolution, human souls
were not yet really individualised, they were still entangled in
the group-soul nature. This was particularly the case with the
more prominent among them ; so that we may say that such
figures as Hector or Empedocles were typical group-soul
representatives of the whole human soul ; Hector grew out of
the soul of Troy, he stands as an image of the group-soul of
the Trojan people.

When [such men] were reincarnated in the post-Christian
time, they were confronted with the necessity of experiencing
the ego-consciousness. This passing over from the group-
soul nature to the experience of the individual soul, causes a
mighty spring forward."

Hamlet stands out as a man in the vanguard of time,
centuries ahead of his fellows, having achieved in
great measure that harmony of thought, feeling and
will which alone can give freedom to the Ego. More
than any other character in Shakespeare he seems

formed to radiate the purest, highest human love. But, though he himself is unaware of the fact, the profound impression stamped in him by earlier incarnations makes him unable to free his mind from the trammels of passionate feeling in all that concerns those bound to him by ties of blood. Government and leadership, in very ancient times, was bound up with the tribal, patriarchal system, in which the ruler or leader was felt as the father of his people, and in many cases was actually related to them by blood. Hamlet, having lived as a pre-eminent example of the Folk-Leader, had become deeply conscious of this patriarchal relationship to his family and to his whole people : a dim shadow of it still survived, as a strong, sub-conscious, protective feeling for all those bound to him by blood, and a sub-conscious tendency to regard the Kingly office as very sacred—both these feelings, though sub-conscious, were far more deeply-rooted and far more noble than the rather superficial sense of family union and family honour typical of his own day and exemplified in the elder Hamlet as well as in Laertes. The story of Orestes reveals how tragic, in the ancient world, was the fate which compelled a man to violate the blood-tie : but the Trojan Hector belonged to a far older civilisation than that of the Greeks, and for him, the flower of Priam's ancient race, the crime of slaying, for any reason whatever, a man at once a King, a near blood-relation and the head of his family, would have seemed a desecration, an act of sacrilege, a deed surrounded by a horror which it is difficult for modern people to imagine. Thus, not only the crime of

Claudius but also the act of vengeance required by the Ghost, might well stir up in Hamlet's soul powerful sub-conscious currents which would break into his consciousness in the form of intensely passionate and yet contradictory feelings, through which his thought could not penetrate, and which paralysed his will. Because he was a man whose conscious attitude to life was essentially that characteristic of our own time, who was accustomed to act not from passion but from reason, loathing the very thought of being "passion's slave," he suffered all the more acutely on finding himself the prey of ceaseless, bewildering, uncontrollable emotion, which would allow him neither to think nor act judicially in the matter that concerned him most nearly. Only at the end of the play, when he sees in a flash that his vacillations have brought about indirectly the death not only of himself but of Laertes and Gertrude, does he overcome his sub-conscious revulsion and perform the deed that not only severs the last link which binds him to the past, but frees Denmark from the danger and degradation of being ruled by a sensual, unscrupulous murderer.

His last words to Horatio reveal the temperate man's feeling that a violent action calls for explanation and justification :

> "O God ! Horatio, what a wounded name,
>   Things standing thus unknown, shall live behind me.
>   If thou did'st ever hold me in thy heart,
>   Absent thee from felicity awhile,
>   And in this harsh world draw thy breath in pain,
>   To tell my story."

The other characters in the play, being as yet untouched by the Christ-Impulse, feel no need to act out of the Ego : they act purely from instinct, convention or passion.

The exact date at which the original Hamlet lived is unknown ; but though the story, in its earliest form, which occurs in the late 12th century "Historia Danica" of Saxo Grammaticus, is laid in a pagan age, it does not follow that the original Hamlet lived prior to the birth of Christ. Rudolf Steiner's explanation would imply incarnation in an early post-Christian century, at a time before the land that is now Denmark had accepted Christianity, and when the "setting" of the events would therefore be pagan. The influence of Christ on the earth would be felt by a very advanced individuality, in spite of the fact that this influence had not been brought into his consciousness, and long before it was embodied in any definite religious form.

Hamlet's tragedy springs from the fact that though, at a very early date, he has developed the Spiritual Soul to a point far in advance of that reached by the average man of to-day, yet in one important part of his feeling-life he remains still bound up with the pre-Christian past. The circumstances of his life force him into a deadly struggle with this one weakness. He dies, having achieved in one life a freedom which the ordinary man only attains gradually, through many incarnations, helped by the normal course of human evolution and the leadership of men such as Hamlet. The tragic anomaly of the survival far into Christian times, of customs and ways of thinking that are essentially pre-Christian, is, consciously or un-consciously, a source of deep unrest to the more advanced human beings ; to these, Hamlet's tragedy has always had a special appeal : the very obscurity which veils his thoughts and motives makes him seem, as indeed he is, near akin to the modern man, who is often troubled by difficulties arising out of his subconscious feeling-life.

The more one ponders on the far-reaching changes which comparatively few Christian centuries have brought about in man's moral and spiritual outlook, the more one feels that Rudolf Steiner's suggestion is rational, and that so mighty a genius as Shakespeare would indeed be attracted to the themes which portray the fate of those leaders of humanity who bore the first shock of the Passage from the Old World to the New. Such a view opens up new vistas of spiritual experience for readers of Shake-speare ; and the fact that it may not, at first sight, appear to tally with all the details that historical research has brought to light, should not discourage either scholars or laymen. The esoteric basis of life may well be more profound than we have hitherto imagined ; and the not too distant future may bring with it the necessity for a complete re-valuation of our ideas and the data on which they are based.

* * * * *

One of the most perfect instances of human love springing from Temperance is the scene, in "The Merchant of Venice," following Bassanio's choice of the leaden casket. In the first moments of their joy, both lovers are overwhelmed by feeling ; but neither speaks to the other until the Ego is again in complete control. Portia says :

> "O love, be moderate ; allay thy ecstasy ;
> In measure rain thy joy ; scant this excess ;
> I feel too much thy blessing ; make it less
> For fear I surfeit."

Bassanio addresses his first passionate outpourings not to Portia, but to her portrait. His actual words to her express great restraint and delicacy. He makes it clear that, in spite of his love, he has no intention of claiming her hand as his by right, merely because his judgment has proved correct ; he still leaves her complete freedom of choice.

> "Like one of two contending in a prize,
> That thinks he hath done well in people's eyes,
> Hearing applause and universal shout,
> Giddy in spirit, still gazing in a doubt
> Whether those peals of praise be his or no ;
> So, thrice-fair lady, stand I, even so,
> As doubtful whether what I see be true,
> Until confirmed, signed, ratified by you."

Portia's reply, considered in the light of the actual relative positions of herself and Bassanio, is a consummate blending of tact, delicacy and regal generosity. She shows a perfect awareness of how he may be feeling, and an instinctive knowledge of how best to mitigate any feelings of embarrassment or inferiority that may, perhaps, mar his joy. Moreover, her love immediately expresses itself in action. With no preliminary inquiries, with no legal safeguards, she hands over to Bassanio her own personal freedom and all her vast possessions—not in passionate self-abandonment, but with a reasoned dignity that makes the act appear perfectly right and natural.

> ". . . the full sum of me
> Is sum of nothing ; which, to term in gross,
> Is an unlesson'd girl, unschool'd, unpractis'd ;
> Happy in this, she is not yet so old
> But she may learn ; happier than this,
> She is not bred so dull but she can learn ;
> Happiest of all, is that her gentle spirit
> Commits itself to yours to be directed,
> As from her lord, her governor, her king.
> Myself, and what is mine, to you and yours
> Is now converted. . . ."

Bassanio's reply shows that he recognises fully the royal nature of Portia's gift, which he accepts, only to change, through the alchemy of love, into a crown for her head. The noble imagery of his speech conveys with delicacy the impression that Portia is a queen, whilst he stands as the representative of a devoted people.

> "Madam, you have bereft me of all words,
> Only my blood speaks to you in my veins ;
> And there is such confusion in my powers,
> As, after some oration fairly spoke
> By a beloved prince, there doth appear
> Among the buzzing, pleased multitude ;
> Where every something, being blent together,
> Turns to wild of nothing, save of joy,
> Express'd and not express'd . . ."

Then, as by common consent, the two cease to speak of themselves, turning, with free, gracious ease, to jest and sympathise with Gratiano and Nerissa. Brief as it is, the scene conveys a strong impression of love conceived as kingly power, self-poised, self-sustaining.

In "Antony and Cleopatra" Shakespeare makes clear the distinction between passion and love. Up to the point of Antony's death, Cleopatra entertains for him an intense subjective fire of feeling, untouched by thought and accompanied by great weakness of will. She deserts him shamelessly in the middle of an important battle, on the result of which all his fortunes depend. Afraid to face his wrath, she sends him a lying account of her own death, a step which leads him to commit suicide, and even when her dying lover is brought to the foot of the monument in which she has taken refuge, her passion, for all its violence cannot overcome her fear of being captured.

> Antony : "I am dying, Egypt, dying ; only
> I here importune death awhile, until
> Of many thousand kisses the poor last
> I lay upon thy lips."
>
> Cleopatra : I dare not, dear—
> Dear my lord, pardon—I dare not,
> Lest I be taken——"

Yet, when she has insisted on causing the wounded man to suffer all the extra pain of being "heav'd aloft" to her, her passion breaks out anew :

> Cleopatra : " And welcome, welcome ! die where thou hast lived ;
> Quicken with kissing ; had my lips that power,
> Thus would I wear them out."

But, nevertheless, when Antony says, a moment later,

> "Give me some wine, and let me speak a little,"

she breaks in impatiently—

> "No, let me speak !"

Antony dies after struggling to give her some common-sense advice, forgetful of everything but the danger in which she stands.

From this point onwards there is a change in Cleopatra. The realisation of his death transmutes her passion into love. Thought and will are suddenly strengthened in her : she resists the temptation to save her own life, cleverly outwits Caesar, and brings about her own death by a very deliberate act of will. The grim humour of her interview with the old peasant who brings the asps emphasises the deliberate, reflective nature of her action.

Cleopatra : "My resolution's placed, and I have nothing
      Of woman in me ; now from head to foot
      I am marble-constant, now the fleeting moon
      No planet is of mine."

With unconscious pathos she dwells, in her dying moments, on the courage she has at last achieved. At last she can act !

      "Methinks I hear
  Antony call ; I see him rouse himself
  To praise my noble act ; . . .
      husband, I come :
  Now to that name my courage prove my title !
  I am fire and air ; my other elements
  I give to baser life."

She can think too, for, in the moment when feeling and will, raised to a high degree of intensity, are fused in one, she remembers her women, and turns to them with unwonted tenderness :

> "Come then, and take the last warmth of my lips,
> Farewell, kind Charmian ; Iras, long farewell."

This power of detachment, this psychic freedom, this capacity to feel deeply interested in the fate of others even at a moment when the sense of union with the beloved is present in great intensity, is characteristic of human love in its most spiritual aspect. Love may vary infinitely in degree, range and intensity : but the quality of love, whether the tension be high or low, is always "rest." This is what distinguishes it from passion, straining perpetually in unrest.

"O God ! I could be bounded in a nutshell," says Hamlet, "and count myself king of infinite space"— and adds significantly, "were it not that I have bad dreams." Another of Hamlet's sayings reveals him as one who knows the secrets of human love :

> "How weary, stale, flat and unprofitable
> Seem to me all the uses of this world."

By "the uses of this world" he implies the customs and habits that make up the round of daily life, so sweet when permeated and sustained by love, so nauseating when the feeling-life is disturbed by some rending shock.

The Englishman's conception of duty is not so much the categorical imperative of Kant as the task of bringing into manifestation, through the slow-moving years, what he has gained through thought and feeling : this is his daily round, his duty. At a certain point in his life he begins to feel that he must no longer take in new thought, traverse unknown regions ; he must fold his wings and begin the sweet monotony of day-by-day existence, in which his maturing will unfolds in action some faint image of what his youth has dreamed and thought. Words-worth expresses this in his "Ode to Duty," making it quite clear that to him Duty is an inner call, a command issued from within by his own Ego.

> "Through no disturbance of my soul,
>   Or strong compunction in me wrought,
> I supplicate for thy control ;
> But in the quietness of thought.
> Me this uncharted freedom tires ;
> I feel the weight of chance-desires ;
> My hopes no more must change their name,
> I long for a repose that ever is the same.
>
> Yet not the less would I throughout
> Still act according to the voice
> Of my own wish ; and feel past doubt
> That my submissiveness was choice——"

The power to create a small world of her own, permeated by inner content, by love, is the special gift of the Spiritual Soul to which Wordsworth referred when he spoke of that "ancient English dower of inward happiness." The whole charm of Jane Austen's books lies in this : that each is a small oasis of peace and rest. The world in which her characters move may be very limited, but it is one of the most harmonious worlds ever vouchsafed to man's imagination, for those who inhabit it succeed in eliminating every jarring note : all who cannot love withdraw, self-banished by their own actions to the outer world, while those who can love draw together in a magic circle of enduring beauty, strength and grace.

> "In small proportions we just beauties see,
>   And in short measures, life may perfect be."

But the very perfection of these books points to the weakness of the Spiritual Soul culture. Human love, at man's present state of evolution, is by its nature comparatively exclusive and limited. Thought begins as a universal principle ; the task of the human being is to bring it into individual manifestation. But human love starts from the individual, and the task of making it as universal as thought must occupy man for countless aeons of time. The human being's capacity for love is still very limited, and no good purpose is served by pretending that it is not. Those who scorn to be bounded in a nutshell, imagining themselves capable of loving a wide circle of people, usually are mistaking the wish for the deed, and find eventually that their palace is built on sand. The Englishman is often unduly blamed for his exclusiveness, his tendency to withdraw into an inner circle of intimates, which he carefully guards from all intruders ; but those who blame him are often persons who live mainly in thought, or in the warm glow of inner, subjective feeling ; who have really no conception of the intimacy springing from unspoken intercourse between "equal souls," joined together in love. Moreover if a man has a natural tendency to perceive and enter into the Ego of another with whom he converses, a certain amount of "virtue" does really pass out of him in the process : if, in return, he receives "virtue" from his friend, a happy balance is maintained and he feels continually refreshed. But prolonged, indiscriminate social intercourse exhausts him to a degree that can hardly be realised by one to whom social life—however rich his thought-world, and however warm his subjective feelings may be—is primarily a means of self-expression ; who is so absorbed in his own thoughts, feelings and sensations that he is not, in a deep sense, aware of those in his vicinity.

But, nevertheless, the tendency to exclusiveness that marks every aspect of English life bears in itself the seeds of a fatal and inevitable decay. The Englishman tends to "stabilise" his thought, feeling and will at far too low a level. He is happy and contented, because he does achieve love, even if it be of a thin, watery kind, but his thought lacks life and vigour, his feeling grows shallow, his will fritters itself away in trivial actions. His nature is such that if he accepts a thought he must assimilate it into his feeling and finally express it in action : knowing this instinctively, he keeps his mind tightly shut, rejecting a new thought as long as he possibly can, clinging desperately to the state of balance he has achieved naturally, without much effort. The same cause makes him shut his eyes and ears to much that is happening around him, lest his feelings should be disturbed and force him to think and act.

Like Hamlet he says to himself :

"The time is out of joint ; O cursed spite,
That ever I was born to set it right !"

The same cause lies at the root of that hypocrisy which is felt—and with reason—to be the Englishman's national vice. Being deeply convinced that his actions ought to be in harmony with what he feels and what he thinks, an Englishman will often invent a lying thought, or simulate false feeling, to cloak a base or selfish action. Clever politicians have long since discovered how to make the people acquiesce in a policy which their moral sense would naturally condemn : they invent some pious lie which may be presented to the nation as a "thought" or a "feeling," and which coincides exactly with the course of action desired. There is, for example, a certain amount of truth in the concept of "The White Man's Burden," but it was used in the nineteenth century to cloak policies which would never have been allowed had the people been made to see clearly what they implied. No nation has deserved more than England the lash that Swift applies to humanity in "Gulliver's Travels," yet even a superficial study of our history shows that when the English people as a whole do succeed in assimilating a true thought, nothing can stop them from embodying it ultimately in action : they are driven by an inner necessity, lying at the core of their being.

A somewhat startling conclusion emerges from these thoughts : that the Spiritual Soul, as such, tends to remain in a condition of "rest," and requires to be roused into activity by some influence coming from without. This stimulus may—and often does—come from the sense-world, or—more rarely—directly into the will from the Spiritual world. It may take the form of a shock to the feeling-life, as in the case of Tennyson :

> "My blood an even tenour kept,
>   Till on mine ear this message falls,
>   That in Vienna's fatal walls
> God's finger touch'd him, and he slept."

Or finally it may come as a new germ of thought. But the characteristic work of the Spiritual Soul seems to be not so much the generating of new conceptual forms, as the assimilating and bodying forth of concepts that are "given" to her—either through experiences or definitely as seed-thoughts.

This is the point at which it becomes important to recognise the close spiritual connection between England and Central Europe. In the German, according to Rudolf Steiner, the pure Ego works with special power : and since, in his "Philosophy of Spiritual Activity," he identifies the act of the Ego with pure thought, one would expect to find in the German, what one actually does find, an intense activity of thought.

We might characterise the special quality of German culture as "self-generated inner activity" ; for music, like philosophy and like mysticism, is experienced "within," and Steiner especially associates this art with the Ego. The most characteristic state of being in the German is one of dynamic energy, a ceaseless striving of the mind. Faust defies Mephisto to make him stop for an instant—never can he imagine himself saying to the passing moment: "Tarry—thou art too fair," as he storms violently through his long life, hurrying with feverish restlessness from one experience to another. The period which marked their highest cultural development is called by the Germans the time of "Sturm und Drang." This mood is reflected in Ballads such as Bürger's "Lenore" and "Der Wilde Jäger"; indeed the German language itself expresses this state through the powerful, stirring rhythms and the short, swift-moving lines, into which German poetry falls so naturally. To an English reader, the verb seems to occupy a very dominating position in German verse: verb-forms, such as present participles, constantly recur. Even a delicate lyric such as Mignon's Song is full of movement:

"Es glänzt der Saal, es schimmert das Gemach."

There is a peculiar pathos in the close of the "Wanderers Nachtlied:"

"Warte nur : balde
Ruhest du auch."

It is remarkable how frequently the imagery of German poetry suggests rushing water; streams, floods, cataracts hurling themselves over precipitous rocks. There is something deeply characteristic of the German in that scene in the Second Part of "Faust" where Galatea sweeps past her father, the aged Nereus, pausing only for a second:

(1) Ner. "Du bist es, mein Liebchen !"
    Gal.   O Vater ! das Glück !
           Delphine verweilet ! mich fesselt der Blick.
    Ner.   Vorüber schon, sie ziehen vorüber
           In kreisenden Schwunges Bewegung."

Then follows the triumphant song of Thales, in praise
of the element Water.

    (2) "Alles ist aus dem Wasser entsprungen !
        Alles wird durch das Wasser erhalten !
        Ocean, gönn' uns dein ewiges Walten !
        Wenn du nicht Wolken sendetest,
        Nicht reiche Bäche spendetest,
        Hin und her nicht Flüsse wendetest,
        Die Ströme nicht vollendetest,
        Was wären Gebirge, was Ebnen und Welt ?
        Du bist's der das frischeste Leben erhält."

Rudolf Steiner speaks of the element Water as an
expression in the physical universe of the etheric
world—the world in which thought is active, and in
his lectures on "Evolution in the Aspect of the
Realities" he describes the reality behind the liquid

---

(1) Ner. : " 'Tis thou, then, Beloved ?"
    Gal. :   O Sire, the delight !
           Nay, tarry, ye dolphins, me rivets the sight."
    Ner. :   Already glide they past, already,
           In a swirling sweep o'er the ocean ! "
                       (Latham's translation.)

    (2) "All things are out of water created,
        All by water maintained.   Thou Life-giver
        Ocean, vouchsafe us thine agency ever.
        If thou in clouds descendedst not,
        The fruitful brooks expendedst not,
        The streamlets to and fro bendedst not,
        In mighty rivers endedst not,
        What then would the world be, what mountain and plain ?
        'Tis thou that the freshest of life dost maintain."
                       (Latham's translation.)

element as "Renunciation." The Englishman descends into the realm of Death, in order to learn the true nature of human Love. What does the German renounce, in the eternal onward striving of his thought ? He renounces the power to bring his whole being into rest, by creating a balance between thought, feeling and will. Faust never achieves love on earth ; his union with Helen is unreal and transitory ; his touch destroys the earthly Gretchen.

At the end of his life, Faust succeeds in uniting thought and will, in embodying an idea in action. Feeling is certainly there, but it plays a subordinate part, being quickly overshadowed by thought. He conceives the idea of draining a piece of land, rescuing it from sea and swamp so that it may become a field of action for some striving, toiling race. Immediately he sets to work, with feverish activity, on the self-conceived, self-imposed, beneficent task, and dies carrying out this final impulse of will :

> "My will from this design not swerveth,
> The last resolve of human wit,
> For liberty, as life, alone deserveth
> He daily that must conquer it—
> Fain would I see such glad turmoil,
> With a free people stand on a free soil.
> To such a moment past me fleeting,
> Tarry, I'd cry, thou art so fair !
> The traces of mine earthly being
> Not countless aeons can outwear."

Not until he is actually in the Spiritual world does he become aware of the Eternal Feminine.

Gretchen, like Faust, fails to achieve human love on earth. She is tender and beautiful, overflowing with nature-love ; a representative of the Soul, but not the Spiritual Soul. Such a being is powerless to resist or help Faust. She falls a victim to his ruthless egoism, bringing destruction not only on herself but on those dearest to her, and almost her last act on earth is to shrink, shuddering, away from Faust, as she sees Mephistopheles at his side. Her mind is broken, distracted, at times delirious : but great waves of true feeling surge up and animate her will, giving her strength to break away from Faust and seize on her own being. She dies an Ego—an independent spiritual entity—freed from the trammels of Nature :

> (1) "Dein bin ich, Vater ! Rette mich !
> Ihr Engel ! ihr heiligen Scharen,
> Lagert euch umher, mich zu bewahren !
> Heinrich ! Mir graut's vor dir."

What she achieves on earth is a union of feeling and will ; only in the Spiritual worlds does she become transformed into a bearer of love, and is united with Faust.

It is significant that there is, in English classical literature, no figure that can be compared with Gretchen. An Englishman finds it difficult to conceive a woman whose nature is flawlessly pure and beautiful, but who is nevertheless helpless, easily deceived, unable to resist or control her lover's passion. Miranda, Perdita and Pamela are children of the Spiritual Soul no less than the Lady in Comus, whose proud virginity

---

> (1) "Thine am I, Father ! Save me !
> Ye angels ! ye holy battalions ! shield me !
> Encamp about me ! To you I yield me !
> Heinrich ! I shudder at thee !"
>
> (*Latham's translation.*)

stands alone, unscathed and triumphant, in the very halls of the Enchanter.

The earthly separation of Faust and Gretchen is symbolical of a real cleft in the German between feeling and thought. His thought is specially strong and active, reaching at its best soaring heights of spiritual grandeur, while his natural feeling is singularly pure and delicate, expressing itself in many forms of true peasant art for which we have no equivalent in England. "Hermann and Dorothea" may be idyllic, but it is essentially a German idyll, springing out of a rich background of natural soul-beauty.

The weakness of the German seems to be that he finds it difficult to bring about a harmonious inter-penetration of thought and feeling. His soaring thought deserts his feeling-life, which, left with only the strength that nature can give, is easily betrayed into false sentimentality ; or, allying itself with will, falls a prey to violent passions. His thought, un-checked, unmodified by feeling, can become inflated, humourless, abstract ; or, passing directly into the will, expresses itself in crude, intellectual "systems," which have no basis in reality. His inner activity can become sheer egoism, all the worse for masquerading under the guise of philosophic thought.

Yet it should always be remembered that the weakness of the German is the shadow-side of his great power of creative thought. He bears the seed of the Ego, and a careful study of the deep currents from which spring the spiritual life of this country would probably show that we owe far more to Central Europe than the ordinary Englishman is

conscious of. The facts that are common knowledge
are significant enough : German music ; German
philosophic thought ; the importance of Luther, not
only in our religious life, but in bringing to consciousness basic ideas that have governed our political
development ; the influence of the Moravian Brothers
on John Wesley ; German concepts of education,
from Comenius onward—for though the latter was a
native of Bohemia, his mind was imbued with the
best elements of German culture.

One reason why the average Englishman is unaware
of the full measure of his debt to Central Europe is
that much of what Germany has given may be fitly
described as seed. It has had to be received creatively,
quickened and nourished by the native soil ; the shape
which it finally takes bears little resemblance to the
form in which it was received. As a nation, we
become aware of the full-grown plant which we have
laboured to grow and which seems—and, in a certain
sense, actually is—our own.

Those who can accept as rational Rudolf Steiner's
teaching that Germany is the representative of the
universal Ego, while England represents the individualised Ego, are bound to recognise that the spiritual
relationship between these countries is of supreme
importance. It might be expressed thus : that what
the German can create as thought, can be "conceived,"
brought down into material existence, by the Englishman—with the necessary reservation that thought
inevitably loses its divine perfection as it sinks into
matter : it can never have, when expressed in matter,
the purity and beauty of its ideal form ; moreover,

the task of bringing it into materialisation must be spread over a long period of time.

There can be no doubt that many of the most thoughtful men and women in this country are feeling an urgent need for a new influx of concepts into our moribund thought-life. In religion, in art, in social science, the out-worn thought-forms of past centuries are no longer adequate : not only are we lacking in creative power, but we are in grave danger of losing all living contact with what past creative epochs have left to us. The actual course of events in the outer world is driving our will, inch by inch, towards a complete revaluation and reorganisation of the social fabric, but unless these mighty, far-reaching changes are accompanied by a corresponding expansion of thought and feeling, the result may be progress, but it will not express the full harmony of human love on earth.

In Rudolf Steiner the true German Spirit, whose essence is thought, worked with a concentrated intensity of creative power. Let England remember this if, in the near future, some terrible shock to her life of feeling and will shatters the pitiful illusions in which she now lives, forcing her into a titanic struggle for existence.

For how does the Spiritual Soul advance ? It is when, through some drastic experience, her feeling swells suddenly beyond the narrow limits of what she can comprehend ; the heart leaps forward into the void. The mind and will fight to establish once more the balance—but at a far higher level. The intellect works with passionate intensity to grasp the full import of the actuality it can no longer ignore, sweeping Heaven and Earth in its efforts to expand, to fill out and permeate the sphere of the throbbing, swelling heart. The will strains and struggles, accomplishing miracles of strength and endurance.

One supreme image stands eternally before the Englishman to express this agonised strife : the figure of King Lear.

CHAPTER V

KING LEAR

LEAR, according to tradition, was an early British king. It is not easy for the modern mind to find a consistent explanation of his action in dividing the realm between his daughters; no other kings have done so, and though there are a few cases of queens abdicating in favour of sons, the desire to retain power as long as possible is such a well-marked human characteristic that it is somewhat disconcerting to find the greatest of Shakespeare's plays based on what might, with justice, be described as a psychological improbability.

For Lear is by no means the type of man who abdicates; in spite of his age, he is full of life and energy, impatient of restraint, accustomed to dominate his environment. Kent says of him: "You have that in your countenance, which I would fain call master." Though he speaks much of his love for his daughters, his treatment of them is cavalier in the extreme; he condemns Cordelia to penury and banishment, the moment she offers the slightest contradiction to his will; he utters an appalling curse on Goneril—whether she deserved it or not is irrelevant, for many fathers who do not love their children so much as to bestow all their possessions on them will nevertheless endure much before cursing them. Undoubtedly Lear would have destroyed both Goneril and Regan in the first outburst of his wrath, if he had had the power to do so. Such actions are not consistent with the psychology of the over-fond parent : Balzac's "Père Goriot" should be studied as a contrast.

Lear's attitude to Kent is not easy to explain : he has no doubt of Kent's devotion, yet banishes him, in violent anger, for the offence of plain-speaking ; afterwards the thought of Kent never seems to recur to him—he dies without really recognising him.

The whole scene of the formal bestowal of his kingdom is an ironical comment on the very act of abdication which is its motive, for Lear cannot even give away his realm without using to its full extent the arbitrary power which he has enjoyed all his life.

Since, as the opening scene implies, the division of the land has been settled already, before the play opens, Cordelia is virtually a princess-regnant : yet this does not save her from beggary and disgrace when she exercises her own will to the extent of giving a reply unpleasing to her father, but in no sense undutiful. Lear's whole subsequent conduct shows that he never intended to deprive himself of power. Cruel as was Goneril's treatment of him, it would not have moved Lear so violently if he had seriously meant the words of his opening speech :

> "'Tis our fast intent
> To shake all cares and business from our age,
> Conferring them on younger strengths, while we
> Unburden'd crawl toward death."

Her conduct was monstrous because, knowing Lear's true nature, she acted as she did.

Judged by the psychology of the modern man Lear's conduct is inexplicable, but it becomes clear if we consider him as one who, in previous incarnations, had lived deeply-rooted in all those feelings that can arise from the blood-tie. In the ancient world, according to the teaching of Rudolf Steiner—and the fact has struck many independent observers—a very deep spiritual bond connected those of the same family, and because of the custom of inter-marriage within the same tribe, family and race were far more synonymous terms than they could possibly be to-day. This was specially so in the case of the ancient Hebrews. Moreover since, through the blood of the father, according to Steiner, Spiritual Beings guided the family or tribe, natural love was in his case inextricably bound up with his sense of the Divine. To understand the agony of Lear we must have some feeling for the concept of the Patriarch, in whom the whole race was gathered up and could rest as a spiritual unity, who was an earthly image of the Father God, in whom His creation lives and moves. Such a sense of Fatherhood must have filled the whole being of Abraham, as he heard the Voice of God : "Thou shalt be a father of many nations," and it ought not to be described as love in the modern sense of the term, being more akin to a natural force, far more noble, more certain in its action, more perfect in beauty and power, than anything man has as yet achieved. It was not a faculty arising out of man himself, but a power implanted in him by God, until he could himself create out of his own Ego the true earth-love, whose Prototype is Christ.

A man who had actually lived as the Father, in the ancient sense, would be more deeply imbued with this divine force than any member of his family : the more completely he had embodied all that was implied in the ancient blood-tie, the more alien to his inmost nature would he find a world in which this force must no longer exist for him. At the core of Rudolf Steiner's teaching lies this concept of Christ : that He alone brought to man that power which makes him an individualised Ego-being, capable of developing love out of his own strength. From the time of Christ's death, the love arising out of Nature ceased to be a motive-force in evolution ; it remained, and remains to this day, as a human instinct, but the true "forward-moving" impulses working in man have, since the Crucifixion, come from Christ. Race is no longer the vehicle of spiritual guidance, having become a purely natural force, borne not by the father, but by the mother.

Those who, in the ancient world, had been the leaders of humanity, had to take into themselves the Christ-Impulse before they could again place themselves in the vanguard of Time, and their greatest difficulty was to free themselves of that which, in pre-Christian times, had been of paramount importance—the blood tie, with all that it implied.

Lear was such a man. His greatness is never disputed. Every word, every action, bears the stamp of a noble, fiery nature ; he has a sweeping amplitude of soul that marks him out as a kingly being, a mighty leader of men. But his strength surges within him ; it is not directed outwards. He acts entirely from impulses rising out of his feeling and his will—not from thought. A leader of the ancient world acted thus, listening for the Voice of God within him, acting as from, and by, an inner force—not from thought, based on observation. Yet Lear is now living in a world from which the Father-force, as a direct, divine, inspiring power, has withdrawn ; it now works only as instinct. He had possessed too much of the Father-force to pass easily to the stage of mere parental instinct, which, when it works healthily, never leads a man to act as rashly and unwisely as Lear did. Balzac, with unerring logic, traced its unhealthy workings, and found them embodied, not in a Lear, but in a Père Goriot—his polar opposite.

Unguarded by instinct, yet bearing within him an excess of powerful nature-forces connected with the blood tie, Lear was placed in circumstances which demanded that he should act as an Ego-being, that he should make full use of his powers of observation and of thought. He could not do so, for in him were still reverberating the powerful echoes of his former incarnations.

It is a striking fact that every single person in his environment—even Gloucester—shows greater power of observation, and more shrewdness, than Lear. Even the Fool is wiser than his Master, and more capable of love. It is as if Lear is surrounded by a cloud which blinds him to the outer world. His personal feeling leads him to judge rightly, but something stronger than personal feeling intervenes and governs his actions. This "something" may best be described as a strong tendency to regard those in his environment—and more especially those of his own family—not as separate individuals, but as part of himself. The two opening speeches of the play strike the key-note of the whole :

Kent :   "I thought the king had more affected the Duke of Albany, than Cornwall."

Gloucester : "It did always seem so to us : but now, in the division of the kingdom, it appears not which of the dukes he values most ; for equalities are so weighed, that curiosity in neither can make choice of either's moiety."

The brutal Cornwall, whose savage nature must surely have made itself felt even through the mask of flattery he would wear at court, is considered quite as fit to have power as the mild and honourable, though vacillating, Albany. Lear has given his daughter to a man from whom he would turn with loathing, if he really "perceived" him. Some dim inkling of the truth makes him prefer Albany : but both men are now his "beloved sons," and, as such, have equal rights. To him, they are not individuals ; they are part of his family. But his daughters are, collectively, the very image of the nature-forces that still sway the sub-conscious depths of his soul, and in them he beholds externalised what once lived in him as divine power. The fact that his children are daughters, not sons, is symbolical of the change that has transmuted the blood-tie into a purely natural force : but Lear does not perceive this. He does not see his daughters as individuals, he feels them literally as his flesh and blood.

> ". . . filial ungratitude !
> Is't not as this mouth should tear this hand
> For lifting food to't ?"

All that in the ordinary man works as parental instinct is, in him, raised to the highest possible degree, and completely penetrates his life of feeling and will, actually usurping the place of his own Ego.

Although the same innate purity and delicacy of feeling that made him prefer Albany to Cornwall, and choose the noble Kent as his counsellor, makes him love Cordelia best, he has no conception of the true nature of any one of his daughters. He never attempts to find a reason for preferring Cordelia, and, though he says he has kept the best third for her, Gloucester's opening speech suggests that he has been scrupulously just to the other two.

Lear's act of dividing his kingdom was an act of unconscious homage to what was Divine in his own past : by this act, he denied, symbolically, the Individual Ego, for in giving the realm to his daughters he felt he was giving it to himself. The idea that they might live and act apart from him, in opposition to his will, never came into his consciousness. He would still be king—in, and through, them ; they stood for something which meant more to him than his own Ego, and in this sense he did indeed love them better than himself. His request, as the price of his gift, that they should express their love for him, was symbolic : they were to recognise and love, in him, that divine Father-force which he represented for them, as they for him. It must be remembered that a son, in the ancient world, brought his wife to the father's house, the marriage-tie being far less important to a man than the blood-tie which bound him to his own family.

Cordelia's reply was a blow to what was most

hidden and sacred in his being, for she bluntly asserted herself as an individual, goaded on by her loathing of the lying words which had given the blinded Lear such complacent delight. The violent passion her words aroused in him cannot be explained, in so great a man as Lear, as the result of mere personal vanity or selfishness. In her spoke the new Ego-force—the polar opposite of the nature-force which still lived in him. The oaths by which he casts her off are as significant as the curse he pronounced on Goneril :

> ". . . by the sacred radiance of the sun,
> The mysteries of Hecate, and the night,
> By all the operation of the orbs
> From whom we do exist, and cease to be,
> Here I disclaim all my paternal care,
> Propinquity and property of blood,
> And as a stranger to my heart and me
> Hold thee, from this, for ever."

Cordelia was not so powerful as Lear, but for this very reason she attained individuality before he did, standing before him in the full consciousness of Self, unblinded by the past. Her perception is clear ; her self-control and presence of mind are admirable. She insists that Lear shall state definitely to her suitors, France and Burgundy, that there is no reason for her disgrace other than the reply she has given. Lear's greatness, his sense of justice, oblige him to grant her request ; and it is significant that the bare statement of her "sin," in plain terms, by Cordelia, acts as a temporary check to his passion. A moment earlier he had described her to the puzzled suitors as "a wretch whom Nature is asham'd, almost, to acknowledge hers," but after Cordelia's blunt and bold reiteration of her fault, in language far stronger than that in which she had first expressed it, he replies only :

> "Better thou
> Had'st not been born, than not to have pleased me better."

From this point it is easy to perceive that obstinacy, rather than violent wrath, sustains him in his attitude to Cordelia.

> "Nothing : I have sworn ; I am firm."

In spite of himself, some dim perception of the truth was forcing its way into Lear's consciousness. It is interesting to note how the Ego-consciousness in Cordelia—and also in Kent—pierces like a sword through the conventional external trappings that enwrap and blindfold those around them. The grandiose protestations of Burgundy are brushed aside, and the man himself revealed, by one cutting remark of the young princess :

> "Peace be with Burgundy !
> Since that respects of fortune are his love,
> I shall not be his wife."

The King of France is suddenly stung into consciousness by Cordelia, and, in a flash, he recognises her in her full spiritual power :

> "Gods ! Gods ! 'tis strange that from their cold'st neglect
> My love should kindle to inflamed respect :
> Thy dowerless daughter, king, thrown to my chance,
> Is queen of us, of ours, and our fair France——"

When Kent says to the king : "What would'st thou do, old man ?" he shows a clarity of perception only achieved by Lear after the agonising experiences which

form the gist of the play.   His last words to Cordelia,
are addressed to her not as a princess, not as a queen,
but simply as a maid.

> ''The Gods to their dear shelter take thee, maid,
>   That justly think'st, and hast most rightly said.''

Lear's division of his kingdom was a deed heavy
with fate : in essence, it was an act of faith in a divine
power that no longer existed.   It has been generally
observed that what has worked in an earlier age as a
prime motive-force, maintaining the health of the
community, tends, in a later age, when it has been
superseded, to become the most fecund source of
evil : that an excess of energy which can find no lawful
outlet tends to become destructive, is true of the
human body, as well as of the soul.   The excess of
the Nature-force in Lear expressed itself, at last, in
his old age, as an act of extravagant folly which let
loose death and destruction in his realm, and which
is stamped by its every detail as rash, foolish, springing
from feeling and will ungoverned by thought.   The
regal splendour of his generosity, no less than the
passionate intensity of his wrath, reveals the range and
power of his soul ; but he is blind to the characters of
his sons-in-law, neither of whom is fit to rule, and
still blinder where his daughters are concerned—
entirely unaware of Goneril's powerful, evil nature,
and the loathsome cruelty innate in Regan. He
indignantly explains that he had intended to live with
Cordelia :

> "I loved her best, and thought to set my rest
> On her kind nursery. . . ."

Nevertheless he banishes her, destroying thereby every chance of redeeming his folly.

But his objective sin is far worse than his treatment of Kent and Cordelia, who are strong enough not to be overwhelmed by their punishment and are more concerned for Lear than themselves. His unpardonable sin is the bestowal of supreme power on Goneril, Regan and Cornwall, the handing over of the lives and fortunes of his subjects to three in whom egoism and cruelty rage in terrifying strength, who represent not the nurturing, upbuilding power of Nature, but her destructive forces, "Nature red in tooth and claw." In them are the ruthlessness and strength of the animal seeking its prey, bent on the one supreme act of self-preservation. By seeking blindly to remain loyal to the blood-tie, not merely as instinct, but as something far more—as a force dominating and ruling the whole man, taking the place of thought—Lear plunged deeply into the dark, evil abyss of Nature. Rudolf Steiner often dwells on the fact that evil is misplaced good. The power that makes the lioness tear the hind piece-meal is the same power that makes her suckle her cubs and defend them at the cost of her own life. Both aspects of Nature are right and necessary, but it is equally necessary for man to be aware of both as Nature-forces, and not be tempted by the moving beauty of the beneficent aspect to exalt it into the place that should be occupied by his own Ego. Wherever man still genuinely needs the support of Nature, she will work in him beneficently as instinct—witness the beauty that still rules and guards the life of the peasant—but when he is ripe to become conscious of his Ego, when, through effort, he could live by thought, then, if he persists in trying to live by feeling alone, by instinct, Nature will turn and rend him.

Lear was potentially an individuality of exceptional strength : his potential powers of thought were great. Potentially he was far in advance of his age, and by developing his thought-powers throughout his life he could have become a quite specially enlightened, beneficent ruler, under whose leadership his people could have leapt forward in evolution. He should have chosen and trained his successor carefully, taking firm steps to ensure that by no possible means could Goneril or Regan seize the power after his death. The fact that his children were daughters, not sons, was an inestimable advantage to him from this point of view, for it enabled him to exercise his judgment freely without departing grossly from contemporary customs.

The main theme of the play is repeated in the tragic suffering of Gloucester : again Nature breaks down into a sheer destructive force. But Gloucester's tragedy is far from being a repetition of Lear's, for he is a man who might well claim to be still under the protection of instinct ; his mental powers are weak, and his sufferings reveal clearly that he is essentially a man who can only live by guidance from without. Even when his natural kindness goads him to independent action, and, revolting from the cruelty of the sisters, he disobeys them in succouring Lear, he has not sufficient courage or decision to defy them openly, and seeks the king in secret. After Cornwall has blinded him, he sinks into hopeless despair : self-destruction is the only idea that occurs to him, and even that he cannot compass without help. Edgar deftly uses the old man's superstition for good, as Edmund had used it for evil. Gloucester's tragedy has its roots in his own youthful licentiousness ; had he remained faithful to the moral law as he himself knew and understood it, he would not have become the father of the bastard Edmund. Nature has not betrayed him in so far as he has kept within the limits of law, for his legitimate son Edgar bears him true filial love, expressing it fully in self-sacrificing action. The opening scene of the play brings the two aspects of the great theme at once into consciousness. On the one hand there is the coarse joviality of Gloucester's references to Edmund, who is present ; a hint of the isolation to which his birth has condemned him ; a suggestion of the painful ambiguity of his position in life. On the other hand, the blind folly of Lear is emphasised by his foolish act, and by his designing to make no difference between his sons-in-law.

Edgar sums up the tragedy of Gloucester in his words to the dying Edmund :

> "The Gods are just, and of our pleasant vices
>   Make instruments to plague us :
>   The dark and vicious place where thee he got
>   Cost him his eyes."

The blinding of Gloucester is symbolical of the blindness which coarse self-indulgence has brought about in his powers of judgment. To claim freedom from law, before the Ego has developed strength enough to rule feeling and will, is to rob natural instinct of its clear gaze, to turn it from a beneficent to a destructive force.

Lear's utterances, from Act I, scene IV to Act IV, scene VI, have at their source this antithesis : the Self, stripped of all its trappings, and the Self identified with what is external, accidental. Lear has insisted on regarding himself as King, as Father. Kingship and Fatherhood are to him aspects of the same Divine Power ; with this he has identified himself, more or less consciously, all his life, and to this identity he clings desperately, torn from it only by an agonising inner strife, his thought eating, as it were, through the living flesh, to tear Lear the Man, from Lear the Father. For as Nature works through the physical body, so too does man's divine Ego, which, although it manifests primarily as creative thought, must ultimately, after aeons of Time, become creative Will in the physical body, even as Nature is creative in man. Lear stands as the great protagonist of the Spiritual Soul ; here in this land destined to become its cradle, he fought out in his own soul and body the great struggle of the transition from the Fourth Epoch to the Fifth. It is in the Will that the Ego engages in its bitterest strife : for there it meets with the powerful remains of Primal Forces which once guarded man, which acted for him in place of his Ego in the ancient, pre-Christian world, and which are externalised and made manifest in the "Evil," that, according to Rudolf Steiner, the Fifth Epoch has to fight and transform.

The first shock of his encounter with Goneril shakes Lear to the depths of his being.

Lear : "Doth any here know me ? This is not Lear :
      Does Lear walk thus ? speak thus ? Where are his eyes ?
      Either his notion weakens, or his discernings
      Are lethargied. Ha ! waking ? 'tis not so.
      Who is it that can tell me who I am ?
The Fool : Lear's shadow.
Lear : I would learn that ; for, by the marks of sovereignty,
      knowledge and reason, I should be false persuaded I had
      daughters. . . . Your name, fair gentlewoman ?"

The idea that Lear's feeling for his daughers had anything in common with the doting fondness of a Père Goriot cannot stand before a careful examination of what precedes his terrible curse. After the bewilderment arising from shock, his mind awakens and gains control of his passion. He points out the lie in Goneril's accusation of his knights. He grasps, in one flash of understanding, the folly of his treatment of Cordelia, the unpardonable stupidity of his whole action, and, striking his own head, he exclaims bitterly :

> "O Lear, Lear, Lear !
> Beat at this gate, that let thy folly in,
> And thy dear judgment out."

To Albany's protestation of innocence he replies, with quiet courtesy, "It may be so, my lord." Then, with deliberate, controlled, purposive energy, he turns to Goneril and invokes on her what was, to a woman of the ancient world, the greatest of all curses —the curse of sterility. The full horror of his words, like the motive force behind them, can only be felt out of the spirit of pre-Christian antiquity. No

modern woman could feel them, no woman of
Elizabethan England could have felt them, as Lear
intended them to be felt.

> "Hear, Nature, hear ! dear goddess, hear !
> Suspend thy purpose, if thou did'st intend
> To make this creature fruitful !
> Into her womb convey sterility !
> Dry up in her the organs of increase,
> And from her derogate body never spring
> A babe to honour her ! . . ."

Goneril scorns both him and his curse :

> "Let his disposition have that scope
> That dotage gives it."

It is only when Lear discovers that she has dismissed
fifty of his followers "at a clap" that he begins to lose
control of his passion. His kingship has been, for
him, identified with its external symbols. The
crown, the regal robes, the anointing with oil—
all these, in the ancient world, had been realities :
living symbols of the divine power which spoke in
and through the king, standing for something added
to the mere man which transformed him into a king.
To Lear, kingship did not lie in the act of ruling a land,
and in giving away his realm he had no thought of
stripping himself of kingship—he was careful to
reserve that still for himself.

> "Only we shall retain
> The name and all the additions to a king ;
> The sway, revenue, execution of the rest,
> Beloved sons, be yours : which to confirm,
> This coronet part between you."

He gave to his sons a coronet, not a crown ; that, with all that it implied, he still retained, regarding it as something inalienable, inherent in himself : a part of his essential being. Like Richard, he might have said, at this juncture :

> "Not all the water in the rough, rude sea
> Can wash the balm from an anointed king ;
> The breath of worldly men cannot depose
> The deputy elected by the Lord."

Nevertheless the difference between himself and Richard is immense. Richard dwells in the full consciousness of thought on these outworn concepts, clinging to them with fond fatuity when all events combine to prove to him their egregious folly. But Lear lived centuries earlier than Richard : what Richard played with as mental toys lived in him as will and feeling, not as thought. The moment thought is stung into activity, there is no dallying with the past for Lear—he turns and rends himself, in his efforts to get free.

Goneril's dismissal of his knights reveals to Lear, in a flash, his own helplessness : "kingship," that magic charm, loses its spell once it is divorced from real power ; it is an empty word. Again his mind awakens to grapple with life : he will go to Regan, she will support him against Goneril—he will win back the power he has given away.

> "I have another daughter,
> Who, I am sure, is kind and comfortable :
> When she shall hear this of thee, with her nails
> She'll flay thy wolvish visage. Thou shalt find
> That I'll resume the shape which thou dost think
> I have cast off for ever ; thou shalt, I warrant thee."

Yet he listens in silence to the pathetic gibes of the Fool.

> "Shalt see thy other daughter will use thee kindly; for she's as like this as a crab is like an apple, yet I can tell what I can tell. . . . She will taste as like this as a crab does to a crab."

The rapid development of Lear's power of perception is brought out clearly in his reply to the knight's remark:

> "Since my young lady's going into France, sir, the fool hath much pined him away.
>
> Lear: No more of that; I have noted it well. . . .
>   How now, my pretty knave! how dost thou?"

Lear bears most patiently with the Fool, whose poor bewildered wits turn round and round his one fixed idea, whose very love for his master can only take the form of tormenting him by ceaseless repetition of his sense of the supreme foolishness of the king's act, expressed with a wearying ingenuity of imagery that might well have driven Lear to distraction. Yet the king never once shows anger, though he winces under the lash so involuntarily and persistently applied. His gentleness, his power of self-control under provocation that to an ordinary man would be unbearable, is consistent with the view that something far deeper than indignation against filial ingratitude lay behind the devastating passion roused in him by his daughters' treatment. The Fool at his side is a symbol of the fact that his folly sprang not from a weakness of the heart, but from a weakness of the head. The falsity of his thought has betrayed him—

this he knows already, before the final interview with his daughters forces him to face the naked reality.

But the final vain struggle with Goneril and Regan, though it tears his soul, releases in him a fiery energy of creative thought. The battle begins, between Nature and his newly awakened Ego. Nature fights through his daughters. She fights also in storm, in lightning and thunder to destroy not only his mind but his body, the Temple of the Spirit.

At last Lear sees himself for what he is : not a Father, not a King, but "A poor, infirm, weak and despised old man." The last words he speaks before his madness imply the full recognition of a new kind of kingship—the kingship of the Fifth Epoch. The king must lay aside his crown, his sacred robes ; he must become a man, but a man strong enough to go forth naked into the storm and strife of life, to feel in his own body the sorrows of his people.

> "Poor naked wretches, wheresoe'er you are,
> That bide the pelting of this pitiless storm,
> How shall your houseless heads, and unfed sides,
> Your loop'd and window'd raggedness, defend you
> From seasons such as these ?   O ! I have ta'en
> Too little care of this.   Take physic, pomp ;
> Expose thyself to feel what wretches feel,
> That thou may'st shake the superflux to them
> And show the heavens more just."

Then, as his thought struggles to create the image of Man shorn of all but his manhood, there rushes out of the hut, by a strange irony of fate, a living symbol of that to which his struggling soul has just given birth—the naked, shivering Edgar, shorn in actual fact of all trappings, all coverings, all disguises.

Within Lear is the concept of the Ego : Man, wrench-
ing himself free from Nature. Before him stands a
human body, naked, exposed to the onslaught of
the elements. His Ego-consciousness is suddenly
intensified, stretched to breaking-point.

Exactly why Lear's mind breaks at this point can
only be felt through the full concept of the Spiritual
Soul, as given to us by Rudolf Steiner : this implies a
clear understanding of the deep relationship between
the Ego of Man and the physical body. Just before
Edgar's appearance, Lear has given evidence of great
self-control, putting forward a sound, rational explanation to Kent of his desire not to enter the hut :

"Thou think'st 'tis much, that this contentious storm
    Invades us to the skin : so 'tis to thee ;
    But where the greater malady is fixed,
    The lesser is scarce felt. Thou 'dst shun a bear ;
    But if thy flight lay toward the roaring sea,
    Thou'dst meet the bear i' the mouth. When the mind's free,
    The body's delicate : the tempest in my mind
    Doth from my senses take all feeling else,
    Save what beats there."

He has deliberately forced his mind to turn from the
thought of his daughters, recognising the danger :

        "O Regan, Goneril !
    Your old, kind father, whose frank heart gave all—
    O ! that way madness lies ; let me shun that ;
    No more of that."

When Kent again insisted on his entering the hut, he
spoke to him kindly but firmly, repeating with dignity
the reason already given—"This tempest will not give
me leave to ponder on things would hurt me more."

Then, realising that neither Kent nor the Fool would take shelter unless he did, he gave way, obviously out of tender feeling for them, for the Fool especially. Every word in this scene, up to the point of Edgar's appearance, reveals that his mind is penetrating, mastering, his feeling-life. No superficial psychology can ever explain why the appearance of Edgar should, in one brief moment, overthrow a mind which the insults of Goneril and Regan had stung into activity and which the utmost violence of the storm had been powerless to shake.

The utterances of Lear in his madness serve to reveal the wealth of the mind that lies broken, and to show that a healing process is taking place : the Ego is struggling to eject the over-plus of the Father-force, and to draw feeling and will into balance with thought. This part of the theme is developed in three separate scenes (III iv, III vi, IV vi.).

In the first of these scenes, Lear's mind dwells on the thought of how weak and pitiable a creature man is, when reduced to his essence, deprived of all that he borrows from the world of Nature.

> "Is man no more than this ? Consider him well. Thou owest the worm no silk, the beast no hide, the sheep no wool, the cat no perfume—Ha ! here's three on's are sophisticated ; thou art the thing itself : unaccommodated man is no more but such a poor, bare, forked animal as thou art.—Off, off, you lendings—Come ; unbutton here——"
>
> (*Tearing off his clothes*).

This image of Man, naked and helpless, he connects with the thought of his daughters : that man should be so reduced, so stripped of dignity, can only come from the denial of the great natural bond between father and child : only the cruelty of his daughters can account for Edgar's state. The truth lying behind this connection is obvious : man's Ego, as Steiner frequently points out, is the weakest, most immature, part of his being. Man's pride in his power to think is the most pitiable illusion of modern life : the world has relapsed into its present chaotic state simply because man's thought is powerless to control the machinery of modern life. He is helpless before the Frankenstein monster he has unwittingly created. The fact that Lear realises the weakness of man is a sign that his shattered mind is struggling to continue the process of re-orientation which began from the moment of Cordelia's speech.

In the second scene, his mind is still concentrated on the image of Goneril and Regan : but he is endeavouring to tear them out of his heart—to cauterise them in his flesh.

> "To have a thousand with red burning spits
> Come hissing in upon 'em . . ."

He has so far separated them from himself that he can sit in judgment on them, and not alone ; he associates with himself, in this judicial act, Edgar, the Fool and Kent. The mad beggar, the jester and the serving-man shall judge Lear the Father : they shall behold his folly externalised.

Then suddenly his own helplessness, his weakness, his loneliness, his pitiable isolation, break on him in full force. Nature in all her manifold forms is no longer part of his being, interwoven with him, upholding him by her all-sustaining power, giving him the illusion of strength and majesty. She is his implacable enemy, urging all her children against him :

> "The little dogs and all,
> Tray, Blanch, and Sweet-heart, see, they bark at me."

In the third scene Lear no longer dwells on the agony of separation from Nature : on the contrary he is filled with a loathing sense of all that is evil, vile, disgusting, in her workings. Here again, sensitive human feeling is in agreement with Lear : it is idle to deny that there is something in Nature which is revolting, ugly, defiling to the imagination. No good purpose is served by pretending that the natural processes are in themselves ennobling, however necessary they may be to human existence.

> "Pah ! pah ! Give me an ounce of civet, good apothecary, to sweeten my imagination. . . ."

When Gloucester says : "O let me kiss that hand," Lear replies : "Let me wipe it first ; it smells of mortality." There is only one brief, but very significant, mention of Goneril—at the beginning of the scene. A few moments after Lear enters, the blinded Gloucester attracts his attention by saying, "I know that voice." Immediately Lear replies : "Ha ! Goneril, with a white beard !" His subsequent utterances show that he recognised Gloucester at once :

> "I know thee well enough ; thy name is Gloucester.
> Thou must be patient ; we came crying hither :
> Thou know'st, the first time that we smell the air,
> We wawl and cry. I will preach to thee : mark me."

Gloucester, the man still in the bonds of instinct, immediately suggests to his disordered mind the image of Goneril, which has now become to him a symbol of something he has torn out of himself. There is no other reference to her.

Lear's mind has suddenly become acutely conscious of the evil in the midst of which he has hitherto spent his life without perceiving it, although it has impressed him in a vague way—much as the difference between Albany and Cornwall, or Cordelia and her sisters, made an impression on his feeling-life without being raised up into the clear consciousness of thought. He knows now that he has fed his heart on flattery.

> "They flatter'd me like a dog, and told me I had white hairs in my beard ere the black ones were there. To say 'ay' and 'no' to everything I said ! . . ."

Gloucester again says :

> "The trick of that voice I do well remember :
> Is't not the king ?"

Lear replies, with bitter irony :

> "Ay, every inch a king :
> When I do stare, see how the subjects quake."

The kingly function is not to wear a crown, but to make full use of the senses, the thought, the feeling, the will : to perceive, to judge, to act. Lear has awakened from his grandiose dream of the past into a present which his long sleep has suffered to grow foul. His kingdom is like

> "the fat weed,
> That rots itself in ease on Lethe wharf."

Lear : "A man may see how their world goes, with no eyes.
Look with thine ears : see how yon justice rails upon
yond simple thief. Hark, in thine ear : change places;
and handy-dandy, which is the justice, which is the
thief :—
Thou hast seen a farmer's dog bark at a beggar ?

Gloucester : Ay, sir.

Lear : And the creature run from the cur ? There thou
mightst behold the great image of authority : a dog's
obeyed in office. . . . Get thee glass eyes ;
And, like a scurvy politician seem
To see the things thou dost not."

It is remarkable that never once in his madness does
he refer to Cordelia, although a superficial psychology
might suppose that he would be, at least to some small
extent, haunted by the grave injustice he had done her.
This in itself is further proof that Lear's relationship
to Goneril and Regan was something essentially
different from his relationship to Cordelia. She, by
her natural development, has freed herself from
him ; she has actually attained Ego-consciousness, with
no apparent struggle. She loves Lear with the true
earth-love, born of temperance, winged with
devotion. It is important to realise that Cordelia
is not a powerful person, such as Goneril. She has
much in common with Horatio, the friend of Hamlet :
both are representatives of those fortunate men and
women who advance steadily, ahead of the normal
line of human evolution : who are in the vanguard,
yet who are not the actual leaders.

In spite of Cordelia's touching beauty, there is a
certain youthful crudity about her blunt reply to

Lear, which, like Kent's manner of intervening, is as tactless as it is well-meant. Like Horatio, she is tongue-tied when her feelings are most deeply stirred —when the King of France declares his love, when Lear kneels before her. When the human being enters upon an entirely new phase of his development, it is easy to conceive that he should find a difficulty in expressing new sensations, new thoughts : that he should have, in a certain sense, to start from the beginning and should only gradually be able to build up adequate forms of expression. Whatever new faculty makes its way into evolution is necessarily hampered by the impossibility of finding, at first, any suitable forms in which to manifest itself, and the same is true of new concepts which endeavour to find their way into the framework of generally accepted thought. The fact is brought home to us in a remarkable way by the revolution that takes place in Lear's manner of speech, when at last his mind regains its balance. Even in his madness he had retained something of the splendid, fiery power of his original speech—rich with stately imagery, moving in sweeping rhythms—the "large utterance of the early gods."

The sign and symbol of Lear's great advance in evolution is that when he awakes, restored, he awakes possessed of power to perceive and love Cordelia in her true being. It is obvious that Cordelia does not recognise him for what he truly is, that she has for him the normal, natural love of a child for a father ; but nevertheless any old man who had been cruelly and unjustly treated, would have roused her pity and stirred her to action in defence of him. A deep-rooted humanity is at the core of her nature. Her understanding and perception are only at the beginning of their development.

> "Had you not been their father, these white flakes
> Had challenged pity of them. Was this a face
> To be oppos'd against the deep dread-bolted thunder ?
> In the most terrible and nimble stroke
> Of quick cross lightning ? to watch (poor perdu !)
> With this thin helm ? Mine enemy's dog,
> Though he had bit me, should have stood that night
> Against my fire. And wast thou fain, poor father,
> To hovel thee with swine, and rogues forlorn,
> In short and musty straw ? Alack ! alack !
> 'Tis wonder, that thy life and wits at once
> Had not concluded all."

There is a poignant contrast between this speech of Cordelia's, so overflowing with tenderness, yet so lacking in any gleam of comprehension for what her father's suffering had been—and the high, controlled passion of the mighty Lear. Both have achieved balance, but Lear has achieved it on a plane infinitely higher than Cordelia's. The gamut of his mind, the range of his feeling, the potential power lying in his will, all are far beyond his daughter's imagination. Yet in her, thought, feeling and will are held in beautiful, delicate balance : she has achieved love. To dwell in meditation on the picture of Lear kneeling before Cordelia is to gain some insight into the heart of love's mystery : how it can be the same, and yet not the same : how human beings can be equal in their inequality.

Like Hamlet, like all who love, Lear can now be bounded in a nutshell, yet count himself king of infinite space.

> 'Come, let's away to prison ;
> We two alone will sing like birds i' the cage :
> When thou dost ask me blessing, I'll kneel down,
> And ask of thee forgiveness. So we'll live,
> And pray, and sing, and tell old tales, and laugh
> At gilded butterflies, and hear poor rogues
> Talk of court news ; and we'll talk with them too,
> Who loses, and who wins ; who's in, who's out ;
> And take upon's the mystery of things,
> As if we were God's spies : and we'll wear out,
> In a wall'd prison, packs and sects of great ones,
> That ebb and flow by the moon."

Like Cleopatra, he associates with the moon feeling that is not love

But Lear is destined to take still one more great leap forward in evolution. He meets Death face to face, in that same deep sense in which Tennyson met him ; for he has recognised in Cordelia the living Spirit, the eternal Ego. His wakening words are no mere wanderings of his delirium : every sentence that Shakespeare wrote, in this, the consummation of his genius, has deep, far-reaching significance.

> "You do me wrong, to take me out o' the grave.—
> Thou art a soul in bliss ; but I am bound
> Upon a wheel of fire, that mine own tears
> Do scald like molten lead. . . .
> You are a spirit, I know. When did you die ?"

This scene—these words—give the key to the full meaning of that mighty climax—

(Re-enter Lear, with Cordelia dead in his arms.)

"Howl, howl, howl, howl !   O ! you are men of stones :
   Had I your tongues and eyes, I'd use them so
   That heaven's vault should crack.—She's gone for ever.—
   I know when one is dead, and when one lives ;
   She's dead as earth—Lend me a looking-glass ;
   If that her breath will mist or stain the stone,
   Why, then she lives. . . .
   This feather stirs ; she lives ! if it be so,
   It is a chance which does redeem all sorrows
   That ever I have felt. . . .
                              now, she's gone for ever !
   Cordelia, Cordelia ! stay a little. . . ."

Lear dies, a pure Ego-being ; a denizen of the spiritual
Earth ; freed for ever from the power of the material
earth, capable of beginning man's task of redeeming
Nature. For a man who, through the power of
Love, has looked on Death, understands the mystery
of the Son, and the mystery of the existence of
Spirit in Matter : he can never deny either Christ or
God the Father.

CHAPTER VI

THE HOLY GRAIL

"KING LEAR" has been described as one of the greatest single works of human genius ; it is certainly recognised as the highest expression of Shakespeare's genius, and for this reason alone it is clear that very great significance must be attached to the play.

According to Steiner the Fifth Post-Atlantean period, the task of which is the development of the Spiritual Soul, began in the middle of the 15th century, although in England it had been heralded in political life by legislation such as the Magna Carta, in religious life by Wyclif, in art by Chaucer. The Elizabethan period in England thus stands near the beginning of a new epoch in human evolution : it contains not only the fine flower of Renaissance culture, but seed-forces of something new, something deeply connected with all that was to evolve in the thousand years following. It is easy to conceive that very advanced human beings, those destined to lead the vanguard of the Fifth Epoch, should have achieved the Spiritual Soul already, while still living in the Fourth Epoch. Through strife, through bitter suffering, their consciousness expanded far beyond the limits that the ordinary man can compass in many incarnations. What Shakespeare expresses in his great tragedies, in "King Lear" especially, is nothing less than the passing over of the Fourth Epoch into the Fifth.

These tragic heroes suffered individually, and in full consciousness, what the whole of humanity has to pass through in acquiring the consciousness proper to our Epoch. But whereas for them the suffering was concentrated into one life-time, for the ordinary man or woman it is spread over many incarnations, and is correspondingly easier to bear. The life of any individual whose consciousness is far in advance of that normal to the age is necessarily tragic : in one way or another such men are tortured by their contemporaries—often unwittingly.

At the beginning of the Fourth Epoch—the civilisation represented especially by Greece and Rome—stands the work of Homer. The destruction of Troy by the Greeks, and the stealing of the Palladium, is, according to Steiner, an Imagination of the passing over of the Third Epoch into the Fourth. But the transition from the Fourth Epoch to the Fifth marks a very profound cleft or break in human development, for which we have no parallel in recorded history. For the Fourth is the last pre-Christian, while the Fifth is the first post-Christian Epoch. Though the descent of Christ to the earth took place during the Fourth Epoch, the first ten or twelve Christian centuries are recognised by historians to be, in spite of their greatness in many respects, "dark ages," times in which what remained of the ancient empires was breaking up while the civilisation associated with modern Europe was still in an embryonic state.

England experienced in a quite special way the transition from the Fourth Epoch to the Fifth. Not only was its name changed, but the inhabitants—an ancient race which had possessed it for many centuries, and whose forms of life revealed the characteristics of still earlier periods—were literally driven out and replaced by a new people, built up out of many heterogeneous elements, whose language shows scarcely any traces of the original speech of the land, and whose national characteristics show that there was comparatively little inter-mixture between the invaders and the conquered. There must still exist in parts of Wales pure-blooded descendants of these original possessors of England, and the people of Wales as a whole are representatives of very ancient pre-Christian races : so that the two countries present a phenomenon unique among Western nations—direct representatives of the earlier and later inhabitants, unmixed, each having its own national organisation, have lived side by side for many centuries. The physical characteristics of the Fourth and earlier Epochs remain embodied in a small group of people who for generations have lived under the same government as the larger group, which is the most out-standing representative of the Fifth Epoch. No other European country presents so clearly marked and so significant a racial contrast ; England and Wales, considered as a single entity, are unique in this respect.

The English people have developed their national life in close connection also with other groups, the Irish and the Scots, in which the Celtic element is either pure, or very strong ; even the Lowland Scots have a much stronger Celtic admixture than the English. Thus the English people are deeply concerned with the relationship between the Third, the Fourth and the Fifth Epochs ; it faces them on every plane, from the most spiritual to the physical, and it is essential that they should grasp what is implied by it.

That some important esoteric "Necessity" is connected with the duality of "Briton" and "Englishman" is suggested by the numerous legends which have gathered around the theme of the Holy Grail. These legends sprang up all over Europe in the closing centuries of the Fourth Epoch ; but for English people the Grail has always been associated with their predecessors, the Britons. It was to Celtic Britain that, according to a legendary tradition, Joseph of Arimathea brought the Sacred Cup ; and when the Britons were driven from their land they left the Grail still buried in some secret place—the English inherited the most sacred treasure of the Celt. A similar idea underlies the legend of the Passing of Arthur : the great King was the fine flower of his race—in him the Celtic Ideal attained its highest human expression. But he, like the Grail, remained in the land from which his people were banished. Again a great Celtic treasure—the living body of the mystic King—was hidden secretly in the land that became the abode of the English.

The Rose of England has its roots in the soil where the Grail lies hidden : the Fourth Epoch has bequeathed its greatest treasure to the Fifth.

It is of the greatest importance that English people should become conscious of the essential differences between the two Epochs ; and should know what elements surviving from earlier civilisations are dangerous to them, and in what lies that spiritual treasure which the Celtic Past has bestowed on them. The subject is especially important at the present time, for the train of external events in the nineteenth and twentieth centuries has brought about an ever-growing influx of the Celtic peoples into England, until now a very large share in the direction of the spiritual, political and economic life of England —both local and central—has passed out of the hands of English people and into the control of natives of Scotland, Wales and Ireland ; a process which, if allowed to continue indefinitely, must inevitably result in the weakening, if not in the destruction, of the English Spirit.

The views put forward by the writer are purely personal, and are not intended to be taken in any narrow, dogmatic sense. They have arisen from a union of concepts derived from Steiner's teaching and the results not only of personal observation and experience, but of attempts to study English literature as an Imaginative picture of spiritual realities.

* * * * *

The core of Steiner's teaching lies in this : that Christ brought to man his Ego-consciousness, the power of self-generated creative thought. Until the coming of Christ, though man had acquired to a considerable extent the faculty of logical reasoning, of deduction, yet he could not produce out of himself an entirely new conceptual thought. He felt that such concepts were either given to him at birth, or inspired into him during his lifetime, by a spiritual power outside himself. This is true even of the great philosophers ; though Steiner makes it clear that very great individuals may have a consciousness far in advance of what is normal for their age, and acquired by means not open to the ordinary individual.

Ancient races always traced their constitution, customs and ritualistic practices, back to some divine being who, in the remote past, had come among them in human form and had carefully taught them what to do. Their pride and prowess lay in continuing to carry out, with minute religious care, the ideas that had been put into their mind from an outside source. Steiner expresses this fact thus : the human being, instead of being guided from within by his own individual ego, was guided from without by high Spiritual Beings, who worked directly into his will, through the blood. A spiritual Being guiding a race in this way acted as a kind of Group-Ego. Instead of carrying out the impulses of their own will, the leaders of the group, or race, were really carrying out the will of a Spiritual Being, and were conscious that this was so.

The pre-Christian race most familiar to English people is that of the Old Testament Jews, who felt that Jehovah himself was guiding them in whatever they did, collectively, as a race. The Old Testament shows that the great leaders of the Jews never did an important action as a result of conscious, deliberative thought. They were told, directly, what to do, and their duty was to carry out the command in spite of their own reason, if this would interfere with the action. The sacrifice of Isaac is the great type-action of the ancient Hebrew. In slaying his son, by all the laws of human reasoning Abraham was doing a deed which would make null and void the whole purpose of his existence, as the founder of a new race. But in spite of the voice of reason, in spite of every natural feeling, Abraham was prepared to act on the direct command of Jehovah.

Rudolf Steiner teaches us that for any great spiritual faculty there must be created a corresponding organ in the human body, before the faculty can become the common possession of humanity. Outstandingly powerful individuals can, and do, achieve the spiritual faculty without having, in the first place, the help of a physical organ ; but the ordinary man needs the physical basis in order to develop and sustain the faculty itself. The organ through which the Spiritual Beings guided the race was the blood. It was through the blood of the physical body that the Group-Ego worked into the will, thus influencing action, and in the ancient Hebrew the blood was so organised that the race could be guided by Jehovah himself ; hence the insistence laid on racial purity, and the frequent repetition of the phrase : "I am the God of Abraham, of Isaac and of Jacob." What was true of the Hebrews was true of the other pre-Christian races ; the difference was that the other races were guided by

less exalted divine Beings—and for that very reason
were less under the control of their Group-Ego. The
extent of the control varied with the different races,
but one might characterise all the pre-Christian races
thus : their blood was so organised that it had the
capacity to receive direct inspiration from the spiritual
world and to pass this inspiration into the will, so that
it could manifest as action in the physical world.

Another basic teaching of Steiner sheds light on the
social fabric of the pre-Christian world. Although
all human beings consist of an Ego working in an
astral, an etheric and a physical body, yet in the male
the Ego and the physical body are the predominant
principles, whereas in the female the astral and
etheric bodies are predominant. Whatever of the
purely physical, or of the purely spiritual Ego-force,
can be transmitted through heredity, is transmitted
through the father. Whatever of the astral and
etheric forces can be passed on, is passed on through
the mother.

In the ancient world, the individual Ego was not
yet active in man as a whole. Instead, he was guided
by the group-Ego, which worked in the blood. The
organisation of the blood depends on the father, and, as
part of the physical body, is spiritually "predominant"
in the male, not in the female. Hence the overwhelming importance necessarily attached to the male
in the ancient world. Spiritual guidance could only
come in a slight degree through the female ; it
was the lofty function of the male to bear within his
blood the destinies of the race, or of his family-
group. Spiritually he was complete without the

female, whose function was almost purely natural and domestic. For the life of feeling—expressed in the astral body—and the life of habitual, day-by-day reasoning—expressed in the etheric body—were, in both men and women, untouched by *direct* spiritual guidance, though they were trained by commandments, precepts and ritualistic exercises. Only the will was directly spiritualised. Since in women the etheric and astral principles, not the will, predominate, the woman of the ancient world was essentially a child of nature, both in her passions and in the workings of her every-day intelligence. In the male the wild passions and animal-like cunning of the "natural" human being were to some extent held in subordination, not by his own merit or power, but by the divine guidance working into his will. In the female Nature reigned supreme, except when checked by obedience to some external command, and she expressed not only its tenderness and beauty, but its cruelty, its manifold instincts of self-preservation.

When any important action was to be carried out the man of the ancient world was constrained to keep the woman in ignorance of it ; her life had to be passed apart, in domestic seclusion. In spite of the fact that a few women, in whom the male element of the blood was exceptionally predominant, could, and did, play important rôles in the national life, it was felt—and with reason—in the ancient world, that for women to gain the upper hand in state affairs meant the denial, or betrayal, of the divine Being guiding the race. It meant that Nature, not Spirit, was ruling humanity.

The whole social fabric of the ancient world was thus a concrete expression of what Steiner puts forward in conceptual form. It was based entirely on the esoteric fact that humanity was governed in races, groups, cities and family clans, by divine Beings who worked directly into the will of the male, through the blood, and who only needed the female to carry out purely natural functions.

But with the coming of Christ a complete revolution took place in the esoteric basis of human life. It is everywhere felt and acknowledged, not only by Christians, that in some mysterious way Christianity changed—and changed with comparative rapidity— the position of women in the social fabric. Just as no thoughtful person can accept the hypothesis that the treatment of women in pre-Christian times was simply an expression of mass tyranny on the part of men, so only a shallow mind can accept the explanation that the change in their position was due merely to Christ's ethical teaching. The work of Rudolf Steiner gives us the possibility of bringing this change —the existence of which no one would deny—into the clear consciousness of thought.

The clue is to be found in his account of the descent of the Christ Being into Jesus of Nazareth, which is described by the Gospel writers as the Baptism by John in Jordan. Christ did not simply unite himself with the blood : he descended into the astral, etheric and physical body of Jesus, filling and purifying every part of these three principles, penetrating even to the bony framework of the physical body. But in filling the human astral and etheric bodies of Jesus, the

Christ entered with purifying power into two human principles which had hitherto remained entirely in the sphere of Nature, and which are especially pre-dominant in the woman. The descent of Christ produced a powerful effect on the astral and etheric bodies, as well as on the physical body : they too became completely spiritualised.

Steiner makes clear the fact that the Deed of Christ was macrocosmic. What was achieved by Christ in the body of Jesus of Nazareth can only be accomplished in mankind as a whole after countless æons of time. The whole earth evolution will bestow on the human race only the Ego itself—the inner spiritual principle through which man is a microcosmic image of God. A further planetary evolution will be required before the Ego can completely penetrate and spiritualise what is now the astral body : a still further planetary evolution will be required for the spiritualising of the etheric body, and only in the remote Vulcan evolution will mankind become an image of Jesus of Nazareth when he bore the Christ in every portion of his being, astral, etheric and physical. Nevertheless the spiritualising work of the Ego has already begun : already some minute portion of the three bodies is permeated by spirit.

The difference between mankind before the descent of Christ to the Earth, and mankind afterwards, might be expressed thus : in the ancient world, spirit could only approach man from without, his own Ego had not become active—now, a spiritual germ, the Ego, is active *within* each individual man and woman. In the ancient world, except in the case of very outstanding human beings, only the will could be penetrated by spirit from without—now the feeling-life and the thought-habits expressed in daily life may also be permeated by spirit, from within. In the ancient world the spirit allied itself directly, through the blood, with the human will, passing over human feeling and human intelligence—now the spirit can only reach the human will by passing first through the feelings and the intelligence.

Those to whom these concepts may appear at first difficult, will easily grasp their significance by comparing the life of a man such as Abraham or Moses with the life of some great man of action of modern times. Columbus, for instance, did not set off to discover America merely on an impulse of will, or because God commanded him directly to do so. He first had the thought that such a continent might exist ; this fired his feeling-life and caused him to begin making inquiries among sailors in outlying parts. It is thought, for instance, that he went to Iceland in pursuit of traditional rumours of the existence of land to the westward. It was only after many years of active effort that he succeeded in firing others with his own enthusiasm ; then he had to make careful plans, involving questions of finance, of personnel, of provisioning. Only as a final result of all these efforts could his initial idea emerge into the will as the act of setting sail across the Atlantic.

Every true act of will, in our days, goes through these stages : it starts as a concept or idea ; it works into the feeling-life ; it then passes to the stage of being planned, organised, by the logical intellect ;

and only then can come forth into the external world with any chance of success. A recent play written on the life of Florence Nightingale brings out these three stages very clearly; any good biographer understands instinctively that he must trace them in the life of his subject if the work is to carry conviction to the modern mind.

The relationship of the macrocosm to the microcosm was a favourite speculation of the Elizabethan mind, and readers of Shakespeare will remember it as the basis of some of his most striking metaphors. Using this concept, one might express the relationship between Christ and the human Ego thus : that the human Ego can and does repeat, in miniature, the macrocosmic Descent of Christ into humanity. Every time a man or woman truly creates a thought by means of his own individual Ego-activity, broods on it in feeling, organises a practical means of expressing it, and finally carries it out in action, he or she is expressing microcosmically the macrocosmic Deed of Christ. It would be true to say that every normal individual does succeed, during any one incarnation, in permeating with true thought some part of his feeling-life, some part of his ordinary, mechanical intelligence, and achieves at least one action which is the result of individual will. Thus, in a certain limited sense, every life may be considered as a microcosmic repetition of the Act of Christ.

Rudolf Steiner makes it quite clear that in every human being, men and women alike, there is a spirit-germ, the Ego, enclosed within the three sheaths of astral body, etheric body and physical body.

Nevertheless, just as, in the ancient world, women collectively were felt to represent the astral and etheric principles—manifesting respectively as feelings and as habits of life and thought—while men, collectively, represented the divinely guided will : so too, in the modern world, the human Ego, which is now the guiding spiritual principle, and the human will, which works chiefly through the physical body, are still to be found manifested more powerfully in the male part of the human race, so that the highest creative thought, and the most decisive actions, are as much the prerogative of men in the first post-Christian Epoch as ever they were in pre-Christian times. No impartial student of history could possibly deny this. It would be difficult to give one single case of a woman's being directly creative in the loftiest spheres of thought or action. The fact that, until recent years, they were denied educational advantages, is in itself proof that they lacked collectively the strong driving-force of a powerful will—for undoubtedly many women in the past did desire a more active life of thought, but were quite unable to release themselves from the network of social custom which held them fast bound. On the other hand, the life of feeling and the ordered economy of day-by-day life is still almost as much centred in women, considered collectively, as it was in the days of the Virtuous Woman described by the writer of Proverbs.

But there is now this important difference : The Ego is the innermost part of the human being, whereas the physical body, the chief organ of the will, is the outermost principle. The principles specially strong in women are "sandwiched in," so to speak, between the principles specially strong in men. Just as, in the individual man or woman, a true Ego-concept must pass through the two definite stages of being brooded over in feeling, and planned out by the logical intellect, before it can emerge as an action, so too, in the body politic, or in any large group of human beings, new thoughts may originate in men, but if they are to emerge on to the physical plane as Christ-like actions they ought first to be received by the women of the community. No action can be truly Christian—in the individual or in the community—unless all four principles are equally represented in it.

The feminine mind, at this stage of evolution, might well be described as the Spiritual Soul, for women have a very special power of "feeling" a thought. Through the plastic forces of the soul they can grasp the thought in all its bearings ; they can brood in imagination over all its implications, all its complications ; they can quicken it into life, embue it with warmth and enthusiasm, with something akin to the powerful working of nature-forces. And finally the power of judgment, the practical common-sense, the mother-wit which enables a woman to make the best use of materials placed at her disposal and which most women are exercising almost every minute of the day, makes her know how the idea should best be organised and inserted into the round of daily life.

One might call the special gift of women "creative receptivity," and it should be used in close co-operation with the "creative activity" of men. There is no question of superiority or inferiority : both types of creative energy are equally necessary for the harmonious working of daily life. Ideally, every human being should possess both in an equally high degree—but since, at the present stage of evolution, our human organisation does not permit of this, every community should so arrange its life that the defect in the individual is neutralised by the harmonious working of the whole. So many of the creative thoughts of men are either abortive, or work destructively in life instead of beneficently, because they are not first "received creatively" by the women of the community before being translated into action. The whole progress of the Industrial Revolution in England—with the financial system that grew up in close connection with it—is an instance of this. Technical science, and international finance, are entirely products of male thought : their application to life, entirely the result of male will-activity.

An interesting instance of the harmonious working-together of the male and female principles in social life is the wide development, in the nineteenth century, of the philanthropic side of medical science. It fortunately happened that, at a time when new discoveries were revolutionising medical work, there existed in Florence Nightingale a woman powerful enough to feel deeply, and comprehend fully, the importance of these discoveries, and of medical work in general. It was through her work in founding and organising nursing as a profession for women that the new medical ideas, generated through the male creative intellect, could be applied beneficently and systematically, on a wide basis, to all classes of the community. Without the steady, loving, systematised, daily and hourly attention of trained nurses, the most brilliant surgical or medicinal treatment would fail.

It must always be remembered that the highest type of feminine power is far rarer than the loftiest type of male creative genius, for the true spiritual development of the great feminine principles was held back until the inception of Christianity and, since that time, has been retarded by all the forces still working over from pre-Christian times. It would be no exaggeration to say that the world has not yet seen anything approaching a truly great woman. It is thus natural that specifically feminine gifts should not have received, at this early stage of their development, a true valuation either from men or from women.

The Elizabethan period is, however, a remarkable instance of a short, though highly important, epoch, marked by harmonious interplay between the male and female principles. It would be difficult to prove that Elizabeth herself actually initiated a single important idea : it is certain that no other woman in her reign was remarkable for creative activity on either the spiritual or the material planes. But the Queen was creatively receptive to a degree hardly yet attained by any other woman, being able to grasp and hold, by means of her spiritualised soul-faculties, everything of importance that was happening in the civilised world of her day. It is admitted that her foreign policy was so involved that historians find the greatest difficulty in disentangling its subtle threads ; but those threads were woven with ease by Elizabeth, and that their final result was something in the way of a consummate masterpiece of political skill is denied by few. In England no important thought could become action without passing through the filter of Elizabeth's great soul. Her male subjects, powerful individualities though they were, were willing not to act until she was ready, till she gave the sign. There can be little doubt that, left entirely to their own will, they would have plunged the country, not only into external strife, but into civil and religious conflicts.

Elizabeth's powerful mind was of the receptive, meditative, judging, discriminating, discerning type, eminently fitted to guide and control the fiery will-forces of the male. The men of her age felt in her a force equal in power to their own, but different in kind, and knew instinctively that by submitting their will to her guidance they were expressing their own Ego in the fullest, richest, most human manner. It has often been pointed out—by Ruskin, for instance—that the women in Shakespeare's comedies and romances display, within their limited sphere of action, a similar guiding, controlling power ; where, as in the great tragedies, the woman, failing to reach the spiritual level of the hero-protagonist, cannot comprehend the problem he is called upon to solve, the man fails to achieve inner harmony, and destructive forces are let loose about him. In this connection, it is important to call to mind one of the most important statements of Rudolf Steiner : the forces underlying the physical body are identical with those that bring about death and destruction in the material universe ; whereas, stored in the etheric body, are life-bearing, upbuilding forces. It is therefore most essential that mankind should maintain a balance between these two principles : when the specially masculine principles are allowed to predominate in a community, destructive energy will inevitably gain the upper hand by an esoteric necessity.

In the time that elapsed between the coming of Christ to earth and the beginning of the Fifth Epoch, the human race was in a strangely equivocal position. The old form of spiritual guidance was withdrawn, especially in the case of the more civilised races ; but the human Ego, in the great majority of men, was still very weak. Moreover the blood of the human being, so far as he remained racially pure, still possessed the natural tendency to unite with spiritual and psychic influences external to man himself. Women, so far from being able to exercise any true guiding or controlling influence, were themselves an easy prey to natural passions and instincts.

Shakespeare's "King Lear" shows clearly the two-fold danger which threatened man in those chaotic ages. As in the case of Lear, he might insist on clinging to the blood-tie : he might persist in regarding himself primarily, not as an Ego-being, but as father, as son, as chieftain of a clan, unconsciously deifying what was no longer the vehicle of a Spiritual Being but merely the expression of the natural racial instinct, which in the ancient world had been rightly regarded as connected mainly with women. This, as explained in the preceding chapter, is reflected in Lear's initial act of giving up his realm to his daughters.

The second danger is exemplified in Cornwall,

Goneril and Regan. The rapacious nature instincts of the human being, as yet unspiritualised by the working of the Ego, might join the blood-stream and work from thence into the will, acting as a direct driving-force which took the place of the inspiration that had formerly come from divine Guides. Then indeed man became little better than a ferocious animal, sinking into unimaginable excesses of sensuality and brutal cruelty. The blood-stained annals of those early centuries can be better understood in the light of these thoughts.

Out of the mixing of the various races, through conquests, through mass emigration and inter-marriage, the Spiritual Powers guiding humanity gradually prepared and built up the new European nations, in whose veins flowed ultimately a blood organised quite differently from that of the ancient pre-Christian races. For it was specially organised to be a physical basis for the expression of the human Ego itself. Man was in an altogether different position when he had obtained a physical basis for the development of his Ego. It now became possible for the average man and woman to become conscious of his own Ego-activity, and to enter upon the task of its further development within the Spiritual Soul. From Steiner's oft-repeated statement that the English were chosen out from the other European nations to become the special bearers of the Spiritual Soul, the writer feels justified in inferring that, in the first stages of the Epoch especially, their blood was best fitted to become the organ of the Ego. It is significant that the English nation emerged out of a medley of races and groups :

its specially hybrid character is reflected in the language, which is far less "pure" than German, French, Spanish or Italian.

It is comparatively easy for English people to become conscious of the Ego : they are helped in the task of developing the Spiritual Soul by the physical organisation of their blood. The fact that they can feel their own individuality in the blood acts as a driving-force to the will : they are impelled by an urge in the blood to express in action what they themselves create as Ego-thought. The same is true of all the modern European nations : but none of these have a blood so perfectly adapted to the expression of the Ego as the English, so that the permeating of feeling and will by thought is more difficult to them. Yet it must be remembered that this very difficulty makes them able to attain greater heights of speculative thought and more profound depths of feeling than is possible to the "temperate" Englishman. The cultural life of Europe would have been thin and poor indeed, had all the other nations been subjected to the development that has been necessary for England. There can be no question of inferiority and superiority as between nations—only the question of differentiated function. Ideally, just as every human being ought to possess in full measure the special qualities of both sexes, so too every person ought to possess the special qualities of every nation—the German's power of inner concentration, the Italian's eye for colour, the Frenchman's brilliant, analytic mind, the Englishman's tolerant good-humour. But since we are too weak, as yet, to develop these qualities without the help of a physical "basis," we must submit to incarnate in the various nations until we are strong enough to discard nationality completely, as we have discarded the ancient system of castes and racial groups, kept pure by inter-marriage. To deny that there exists any difference whatever between nations, holds back the natural course of evolution as surely as to deny that differences, other than physical, exist between men and women. On the other hand, to exaggerate the importance of these differences is still more reaction- ary : the eternal Spirit of Man transcends all differences of race, nation or sex—these are transitory forms, aids to progress, which will vanish in proportion as man outgrows them. Man best learns to outgrow them by facing them with frank courage, in the clear consciousness of Ego-thought, and by taking the fullest advantage of the rich diversity of life which is made possible to him by the existence of these different cultures and gifts.

Among the Western people, the Celt occupies a quite special position. Considered racially, he belongs to the pre-Christian Epochs. He has less "support" for the development of his Ego than any other Western group, for his unmixed blood is not adapted to be the expression of his individuality : he receives little or no help in achieving the Spiritual Soul from his physical organisation. A largely Celtic race, left undisturbed in the Highlands of Scotland, continued to maintain right into the eighteenth century a whole system of life quite unsuited to the Fifth Epoch, and really based on the tribal, patriarchal system characteristic of pre- Christian Epochs. The break-up of this system came from the pressure of external events rather than from the initiative of the people themselves. To a greater or less extent, traces of this clan or "family" system remained till an abnormally late date among all those in whom Celtic blood is strong : even the history of the Scottish Lowlands shows what an important part was played by the feuds and rivalries of great families, which weakened the government of the country. Those in whom Celtic racial characteristics are strong find a quite special difficulty in resisting all the manifold forms of nepotism—a weakness which must inevitably bring about the collapse of any social fabric in which it is allowed scope.

The Celt is further handicapped in the Fifth Epoch by the fact that his blood still retains a tendency to unite with astral and spiritual influences not emanating from his own individuality. When this happens, he is indeed driven by an urge in the blood which he, and others, easily mistake for his own will-force, but which is really a medley of racial and "family" instincts ; or an occult force, unrecognised, yet none the less dangerous. The Celt is, by his very physical organisation, eminently adapted to be the medium—often the innocent medium—of those who desire to cling to decadent spiritual forces left over from earlier Epochs, while making full use of the external framework of society built up by the Fifth Epoch. He tends to form, and to impose on others, a false estimate of his own powers, when he feels stirring within his blood the "natural" strength and glory of his whole race. There is no danger whatever in an innocent expression of racial pride, if it is recognised for what it is—but there is danger if pride of race is regarded by the man himself, or those who have to deal with him, as an indication of individual merit or ability.

Steiner teaches that, as the modern European nations were created, Beings of the Hierarchy of the Archangeloi undertook the task of guiding them ; he describes a modern nation as a community living under the guidance of an Archangel. But the Folk-Spirits of the Fifth Epoch do not work directly, from without, on the human will ; their inspirations must be received freely into the feeling and thought life of the people they are guiding, and from thence pass into the will— thus their guidance, besides being indirect, depends to a great extent on the free will of the individuals composing the nation—on whether they can accept, and use in the right way, the inspiration coming from their Archangel.

In so far as race and nationality are inherited through physical descent, they are transmitted through the feminine principles ; they ought not to rage as passions in the blood of the male, which should now be the bearer of the individual Ego. A man who falls a victim to race-passion of any kind is denying his own Individuality. The economic sphere, connected as it is with the human will, should already be freed from all national or racial bonds. Race and nationality should find rich and peaceful expression in the language and art of a country, in its characteristic ways of thought, in its customs and in its institutions. Expressed freely in these spheres, they would never lead to strife. Strife between nations occurs when the blood of the male is directly dominated by some force—racial or occult—other than his own Ego, so that his will is paralysed or perverted. The economic sphere, which, according to Steiner, is specially connected with the human will, is most certainly not ruled by man's Ego at the present time. On the contrary man is dominated by economic "forces" against which his will appears powerless. The very jargon of Finance, with its sinister personification of abstractions such as "British Interests," is a testimony to something evil at its core. There are no British Interests—there are only the interests of the individual man or woman. These so-called "British Interests" are, in plain fact, merely the interests of a few individuals and do not benefit in any way the rest of the citizens of the Empire. The use of the word "British" however, masks very cleverly the egoism of the individuals concerned, raising it to the status of lofty patriotism. This points to the danger connected with nationality in our Fifth Epoch. It may be deliberately used to hide reality : behind the stately facade of Empire or Kingdom or Republic certain individuals are wielding, for their own pleasure and profit, a power which would certainly be torn from them if the masses of the people were not still easily deceived by the gorgeous trappings left over from the earlier Epochs. The fact that national differences do actually exist, in spheres other than that connected with the will, makes the task of deceiving the people more easy. Exact esoteric knowledge is becoming more and more necessary, to combat the deliberate misuse and misrepresentation of such human realities as race, nationality and sex. At present, for lack of such knowledge, well-meaning men and women are fighting in the dark, wasting their strength and courage, often doing harm where they imagine they are working for good. On the other hand, those who wish to obstruct evolution are well aware of much that the ordinary man and woman ought to know also—the sooner this fact is grasped, the better will it be for humanity at large.

One might sum up briefly those elements carried over from the earlier Epochs which ought never to be allowed to influence the course of affairs in the Fifth : the enhancement of the personality through "pride of race" : tendencies towards nepotism, in any form : the allowing of personal or "family" ambition to work like a kind of physical passion in the blood—the tragedy of Shakespeare's Macbeth : the allowing of bad occult forces to work upon humanity by directly influencing the will.

In "King Lear," Shakespeare shows all these evil forces working with demonic energy, bringing moral ruin and social havoc in their train.

The writer has no intention of suggesting that these Fourth Epoch characteristics have survived only in the Celt—this would be obviously untrue. But English people do receive considerable help, in overcoming them, from their physical organisation : their predominating weaknesses arise out of Fifth Epoch conditions. It is a recognised fact that no Celtic people succeeded out of its own initiative in building up a social fabric suitable for the Fifth Epoch, or even in achieving a sufficient measure of national unity to resist invaders—the rise of Holland and Switzerland show that even very powerful external attacks fail against a united people, however small.

The English, on the other hand, have shown a special genius for the building up of a social framework suitable for the Epoch—a framework which the individual Celt himself has found most congenial for the development of his own admittedly brilliant gifts. It is surely not unreasonable to suggest that, while the Celt has every right to autonomy in his own lands, and the freedom of the Empire, the truest interests of the whole British Commonwealth will be best served if the guiding and directing of life in England itself is in the hands of English men and women.

In the great figure of Lear himself Shakespeare shows the human Ego overcoming all physical hindrances, tearing aside every veil of passion, fighting its way towards complete, victorious self-recognition. Lear the Celt stands out as the great Protagonist of the Ego ; in spite of the physical and psychic handicaps imposed on him by his ancient race, he achieved the Spiritual Soul centuries before the dawn of the Fifth Epoch. Cordelia also, in early youth, has already freed herself from the domination of the Fourth Epoch. But it is significant that Cordelia is helpless in the outer world, she has none of the power that surges in Goneril. The King of France takes her under his protection : it is he who lends her an army with which to rescue Lear. Lear himself, when his blood is purged of what remained over from earlier incarnations, is filled with a desire to withdraw from the outer world. He no longer wishes to dominate, to rule externally : he wishes to look on at life from a sheltered place where he and Cordelia may live at peace. The defeat of Cordelia's army, and the helplessness of both Lear and Cordelia in the hands of Goneril, are significant.

The highest type of Celt, whose blood remains pure of racial passions and instincts, can, and does, achieve the Spiritual Soul to a high degree : but at the same time he becomes conscious of a certain powerlessness in the outer world. In proportion to the real strength of his Ego, he is not effective in the domain of will. He has no urge in his blood to spur him on in the fight against material difficulties : he has no desire whatever to dominate his environment : he has to force himself, against the grain, to enter public life. His Ego works all the more powerfully in the spheres of feeling and thought. The Celt of this type is often a brilliant and original thinker, or inventor : he is singularly pure and impartial in all his judgments, unworldly and disinterested to a high degree. The very fact that his Ego does not find its full expression in action only makes him more "inward," more subtle and profound, more inclined to mysticism. If England owes much to German Thought, she also owes much to the highest type of Celt, who brings into her cultural life an element from which the Englishman, with his gaze turned outward towards the material universe, is to a great extent debarred. Milton intuitively perceived this Celtic clarity of spiritual vision, and expressed it imaginatively in the figure of his river-nymph, the Celtic Sabrina, whose cool, pure touch alone has power to free The Lady from the spell of Comus.

Yet the loftiest symbol associated with Celtic

Britain is a physical element, part of the human body itself. Shakespeare, in the figure of Lear, stresses neither the mysticism nor the imagination that are commonly regarded as the highest gifts of the Celt— what he does show with great power is the titanic struggle of the Ego to drive out of the blood all the ancient racial passions which were governing and perverting the actions of the King. When Lear had cast out of himself all that was represented by Goneril and Regan, his blood remained spiritually pure. It was not, like the blood of the modern man, of the Englishman especially, the physical organ of his Ego : it was no longer used by a Spiritual Being as an instrument for guiding the race : it was no longer dominated by astral passions. It was an element brought over directly from pre-Christian times, made and kept pure, from within, by the action of the human Ego—yet still retaining the potentiality of receiving impulses from the spiritual world.

The Blood of the Grail was, according to tradition, part of the body of Jesus of Nazareth, transmuted by the indwelling of the Christ, and afterwards left as a perfectly pure divine element, untouched, unsullied by any human impulse.

Imagination, rather than reason, can perceive that the new nations of the Fifth Epoch, by descending into the physical body, have lost the possibility of a certain unsullied spiritual purity of the blood, which the Celt in the closing years of the Fourth Epoch still felt to be a possibility for himself. If he could succeed in conquering with his Ego all the racial instincts and natural passions which presented so great a temptation to him, then his blood might become a pure receptive element—a kind of earthly, human image of the Divine Blood of the Grail itself. Thus the quest of the Grail came to represent the highest Ideal of the Celt : he sought the spiritual purity of the blood, by self-conquest and self-recognition. This pure element, he felt, was destined to be of use to those who, in the distant future, would no longer possess the highest gift of the pre-Christian races—the power to receive directly, into the physical body, the Will of Spiritual Beings far loftier than man himself.

It is the German Wagner who, more than any other man, has brought the image of the Holy Grail into the modern consciousness. Steiner spoke of him as an artist whose creations flowed from an initiated consciousness ; the aspect of this theme which Wagner chose to make the subject of his great work must be of special significance to our world. The function of any great artist is to light up the mass of amorphous material accumulated through the ages, so that the ordinary mind may see what part of the past has living meaning for the present.

As presented by Wagner, the Holy Grail is guarded in a remote place by Amfortas and the Knights of his Order. The direct impulse of the Holy Spirit does not reside perpetually in the Grail ; but, when it is unveiled by the priestly Guardian, "A dazzling ray of light falls from above upon the crystal Cup, which now glows ever deeper . . . shedding a soft light on all around."

The Holy Grail is two-fold : the Cup and the Blood within it. It had been brought to Titurel by angels.

"To him, as threat of savage foeman's might
   The realm of holy faith distressed,
 Once, bending down to him in solemn night,
   Appeared the Saviour's messengers blessed ;
 Whence last He drank, who Feast of Love ordained,
 That holy Cup, the Vessel unprofaned,
 Which at the Cross His Blood divine received,
 Therewith the sacred Spear, His wound that cleaved—
 This witness-treasure, wondrous high and rare,
 Was placed by angels in Titurel's care."

It is the Blood which receives the ray of light from
heaven and which glows with divine power through
the sacred Cup. For this physical element, part of
the human body of Jesus of Nazareth, transmuted by
the indwelling of Christ, has the capacity to be the
bearer of the Holy Spirit. From time to time the
Holy Spirit can descend and work from thence directly
into the world of human beings, through the Grail
Knights, who are made strong by the unveiling of the
Cup.

Rudolf Steiner explains that the failure of Amfortas,
and the transference of the guardianship of the Grail
from him to Parsifal, is symbolic of the spiritual
passing-over of the Fourth Epoch into the Fifth ; for
Parsifal is representative of the Spiritual Soul : his
feeling-life, purified and strengthened by the Ego
working within it, can withstand the temptation of
the flesh which mastered Amfortas. The transforma-
tion of Kundry is an outer manifestation of the change
within the Soul.

During the years between the first appearance of
Parsifal—the dawn of the Spiritual Soul—and his
return, with matured powers, Amfortas has been

unable to unveil the Grail ; the knights have remained unstrengthened by divine Grace ; the power of the Order has declined. But when Parsifal unveils the Grail and kneels in prayer before it, the ray of light again falls from above : the Holy Spirit can again descend into the sacred Blood.

Rudolf Steiner makes clear that it would be a serious error to regard the Temple of the Grail as actually on the physical earth. Both Temple and Grail are of a purely spiritual nature—they never descend to the earth plane. But, nevertheless, the Grail may be considered as a Symbol. Since the blood is the physical element in which is expressed the human Ego : and since the Ego reveals itself in the physical body as will : we are justified in regarding the Holy Grail as a Symbol representing divine Inspiration descending into the human will. The Cup which bears the Blood represents, according to Rudolf Steiner, the Virgin Soul : the Cup is an essential part of the Grail—for no divine Impulse can work into the will without the mediation of the purified Soul, the divine feminine.

While Wagner was thus inspired by the most universally spiritual aspect of the Grail story, his English contemporary, Tennyson, was seeking to embody in verse that other legend, which is closely connected with the Grail story, and which may be regarded in some respects as a translation of the universal Symbol into earthly actuality—the story of Arthur.

As the Grail itself, according to Celtic legend, was buried in the neighbourhood of Glastonbury, so the living body of Arthur was hidden in some secret valley of the same region. The physical body of Arthur was felt as an important element, something which had to be preserved, carried over into the future. Arthur's power to work in the world, at the time of his promised re-appearance, would seem to depend on the continued existence of that earthly "vehicle" which really belonged to the pre-Christian Epoch, and which only by a special mercy, a special gift of Heaven, was allowed to "pass" into the Fifth Epoch.

CHAPTER VII

KING ARTHUR

In spite of the theological controversy that surrounded the birth of Protestantism, it would be true to say that the Christian Impulse which made its way into the world mainly through the instrumentality of Luther was received by the feeling-life of the people rather than by their thought. The modern mind, reading the doctrinal teachings of the English Puritans, for example, is struck by their crude naïveté; Bunyan's "Pilgrim's Progress" reveals how weak was the thought-foundation on which rested the Protestantism of the average Englishman. Christian is accompanied on his way by Faithful and Hopeful, but there is no Thoughtful to guide his steps, though he is strongly endowed with robust commonsense. Charity remains secluded in the House Beautiful; unlike her sister, she is not represented in the outer world of the Pilgrimage itself. This remarkable fact, rightly understood, throws light not only on Puritanism, but on all forms of Protestantism, explaining what many critics have deplored, and what cannot be denied—that Protestantism, from its very inception, has been strangely mingled with the hard, grasping, ruthless system of finance and economics which has grown up with the modern world.

Luther himself upheld Faith as fundamental, basic, to true Christianity : nothing could save a man but a deep inner conviction of the working of Christ within his individual soul. Something must light up in his feeling which could give him the same certitude that in the realm of daily life he could only derive from the exercise of sense-perception and judgment. The Diary of John Wesley shows that the whole object of his life was to awaken this living Faith in every man or woman with whom he came into contact : to this day the Evangelical Churches, and other religious bodies, have this aim ; while those Churches which rely on Sacraments endeavour to awaken Faith through ritual.

Faith is connected with the personality : it is expressed not by logic, but by the feeling behind the logic : not in what a man says, but in the tones of his voice, the attitude of his body. The magnetic feeling that animates him can pass like a current into the feeling-life of those in his vicinity. That is why the spread of Protestantism, in its first stages, has been so closely bound up with the spoken word. It is the great Preachers who have stirred the people—men whose collected sermons, read judicially in cold blood, can give little conception of the living flame that burned within them, firing the hearts of their hearers.

Many who, feeling themselves to be sincere Christians, approach the writings of Rudolf Steiner, may at first be repelled because they do not find in them that direct appeal to Faith which they have always associated, and rightly, with the great teachers of Christianity. Steiner quite consciously refrained from any direct appeal to the feelings, for his whole mission was to carry Christianity into the thought-life.

If, in Luther and his great co-operators, a new Impulse from Christ may be said to have descended into the astral body, into the feeling, it may be said that in and through Rudolf Steiner, this same Impulse has descended into the etheric body. He has made it possible for man to grasp in thought aspects of Christianity which, up to now, have been held reverently in the darkness of the feeling-life.

It is important that leaders of Protestantism should be willing to face the fact that the thought-basis underlying their Faith has been weak. Newman revealed the inherent weakness of the thought-structure on which rests the Anglican Church. The brilliance of his intellect drove him to Rome. For though the Roman Church has discouraged the layman from thinking for himself, its theology has been built up on logic : for sheer intellectual brilliance, Thomas Aquinas and many of the great Scholastics remain unsurpassed—as Professor Whitehead, among others, acknowledges.

There has never been a more sincere Protestant Christian than Samuel Johnson : his powerful personality did for the cultured classes of eighteenth century England what John Wesley did for the masses : he upheld the fire of living Faith in their hearts, holding back from England the tide of atheistic free-thought which was sweeping over France and Central Europe. His importance to England—and hence to the world —can hardly be over-estimated. But Johnson only achieved Faith by sacrificing logic ; the following passage is typical of the man's whole attitude :

"One evening, when a young gentleman teased him with an account of the infidelity of his servant, who, he said, would not believe the Scriptures, because he could not read them in the original tongues, and be sure that they were not invented, 'Why, foolish fellow,' said Johnson, 'has he any better authority for almost everything that he believes ?'

Boswell : 'Then the vulgar, Sir, never can know they are right, but must submit themselves to the learned.'

Johnson : 'To be sure, Sir. The vulgar are the children of the State, and must be taught like children.'

Boswell : 'Then, Sir, a poor Turk must be a Mahometan, just as a poor Englishman must be a Christian ?'

Johnson : 'Why, yes, Sir ; and what then ? This now is such stuff as I used to talk to my mother, when I first began to think myself a clever fellow ; and she ought to have whipped me for it.''

It is clear that so long as a man's thought is limited, concerned only with the events and problems of his personal life, a Christianity based on Faith can be sufficient for his needs. But when his thought begins to travel in a wider circle ; when he begins to face problems involving the destiny of whole races and nations—then Faith alone becomes more and more inadequate.

The rapid growth of science during the 18th and 19th centuries suddenly enlarged man's mental and physical horizon ; the 20th century has multiplied his responsibilities, stretched his world till it is commensurate with earth herself; but Christian teaching has remained, in essence, at the stage of the 17th century. Its conceptual basis did not expand sufficiently to "comprehend" the new scientific concepts. Faith is no longer in any direction commensurate with knowledge. No good purpose is served by Christians' ignoring this fact. Tennyson's "In Memoriam" was the last great artistic expression of Faith : but in essence it is a prayer to God, that He will vouchsafe to man new knowledge of His Being. Faith, in Tennyson, became transformed, through will, into a Prayer for Enlightenment.

Protestant England turned to the German Spirit for the Impulse which finally crystallised into form the new Faith that from the time of Wyclif had been stirring vaguely in her soul. To-day, new ideas are stirring vaguely in her thought-life : let her turn again to the same source for the Christ-Concepts she needs, to quicken into new, vigorous life her people, who are sickening, dying of sheer intellectual inanition.

To neglect to study the whole work of Rudolf Steiner, at this moment of time, is to miss the clue which alone can guide us through the labyrinth of contemporary events. A heavy responsibility rests on the leaders of Christianity if they continue to preach Faith alone to a world which is crying out for new spiritual knowledge, and which will assuredly perish if the requisite knowledge is not forthcoming.

But when the Christian Impulse has descended through the feeling-life, into the thought-life, there is still a third stage : it must manifest as will in the material world. No sincere Christian would claim that anything but a small portion of what Christianity stands for has yet been manifested objectively in the outer world. The whole basic construction of modern society is a denial of Christ on earth, in spite of the fact that individual Christians have, by personal effort and sacrifice, done much to mitigate the evil arising from the working of the system as a whole. Love has undoubtedly manifested itself, in rich measure, in the sphere of personality : man has succeeded in letting his balanced thought, feeling, and will pour outward towards some other individual human being. But if the new Christ Impulse which began with the Reformation descended into the human will, in as full a measure as it descended into the feeling-life at its inception—when large numbers of men and women would rather be burnt alive than deny their Faith—then love would be reflected, not only in the personal relationships of individual human beings, but in the whole organisation of society.

A social fabric which reflected love would be based, not on the economic domination of the many by the few, not on the forced toil of people whose labour-power, regarded by society as a commodity, is bought and sold in the market, just as formerly slaves were bought and sold : whatever its external form, the essential basis of such a society would be human freedom, the voluntary services which men and women of goodwill give to the community— not because they are driven by economic compulsion, but because they desire to serve their fellow-men.

It is clear that many human beings are still far from the stage at which such a standard of conduct is natural to them ; but this matter should be considered positively, not negatively. Are there enough people in England with sufficient good-feeling towards their fellows to begin the building up of such a society ? It should be remembered that the full utilisation of the mechanical resources of the nation—now deliberately held in check by the financial rulers—would do away with the necessity for much of the heaviest drudgery and would easily produce sufficient material wealth for the needs of all.

The question might be put in another form : Are there enough Christian men and women in England to begin such a task ? Is there enough faith in the divine origin of Man ? Is there enough faith in the dynamic love-power of Christ ?

It is not a question of whether the masses of the people can be suddenly and simultaneously imbued with a Christianity, the evidences of which have been tragically lacking in the society into which they have been born : rather, the goal of the new society would be to lead the masses by example, not precept, to believe in the power of Christian love. It is a question of whether those men and women of all ranks and classes who are now professing Christians, can band themselves together in love to receive creatively the mighty inflowing of the Christ-power, which could then pass like a current through this land, pouring through innumerable channels, giving strength to the weak and sight to the blind.

There is a passage in St. Matthew which is of great significance to those whose duty it is to unfold the Christ-Will on earth :

"Verily I say unto you, Whatsoever ye shall bind on earth, shall be bound in heaven : and whatsoever ye shall loose on earth shall be loosed in heaven.

"Again I say unto you, That if two of you shall agree on earth as touching anything that they shall ask, it shall be done for them of my Father which is in heaven.

"For where two or three are gathered together in my name,
there am I in the midst of them."

Until the year 1919, the Idea of a Christian Society,
suitable for our Fifth Epoch, had not been given to
man. But in 1919, Rudolf Steiner published in
Germany his book "The Threefold Commonwealth"
(translated into English in 1920), in which he set forth
the Idea of a modern Christian State.

In 1919 also, Major C. H. Douglas, working along
quite different lines, finished his book "Economic
Democracy," in which he first gave to the world his
discovery of the flaw in the working of the existing
financial system, and the means whereby this defect
may be remedied.

If these two books, which appeared almost simultaneously from two entirely different and independent
quarters, are studied in conjunction, it will be seen
that there is a relationship between them. Steiner
gives the complete Idea of a Christian State : Douglas
shows us how to take the first great step towards
converting this Idea into reality. Steiner says :
"The spiritual being of man must be set free from
economic compulsion." Douglas shows how the
existing financial system might be rapidly transformed so that every man and woman could actually
be set free to work for the community.

One might say that the Social Credit Theory of
Major Douglas is the means by which the Ideal
Picture, given by Steiner, may *begin* the long process
of its descent into the plane of external reality.

Yet neither Idea nor Theory can, of themselves
alone, become reality : only if the Soul of the people

receives them creatively can they reach the human will. All English Christians, and English women especially, bear a heavy weight of responsibility at this moment of time. It is their duty to grasp, to comprehend, what Steiner and Douglas have put into the world of thought. They must feel and understand the Christ-Concept of Steiner, and the practical Theory of Douglas. Unless and until they do this, neither Concept nor Theory will be able to reach the will, and pass directly into action. The will of England is paralysed, because the Soul of England is asleep—not, as yet, impure or incapable of thought, but sunk in lethargy, dissipated in the pursuit of unimportant personal interests, blind to what is happening in the objective world. Let English women once awaken to a sense of duty, to a knowledge of the lofty part they must play in the life of the nation, and this country will be saved from the creeping death that is now destroying it daily.

The Concepts of salvation are here in the world : the men of the nation possess sufficient will-power to carry them on to the plane of external life. But the Spiritual Soul must give the sign, before this power can enter into activity. So far, these concepts have not been received with living warmth into the feelings : they have stirred neither the imagination nor the heart, for the majority of those who have accepted them have received them into the dry, abstract, logical intellect.

Women are capable of comparatively little direct action in the objective physical world : but they possess that type of imagination which can picture vividly the sufferings and wrongs of humanity, they have hearts which can feel intense sympathy for that suffering, and they have a strong ethical sense which should make them abhor the cruelty of an economic system that destroys, ruthlessly and continuously, not only food and goods of all kinds but the life and happiness of countless human beings.

Considered collectively, the women of England stand for the Soul of England : and thoughts so vast in their import that they concern the whole nation must pass through that Soul, before they can be translated into action—although there may be few externally visible signs of its passage.

If England fails the world, at this crucial point in history, it will be through the intellectual sloth, the stultified imagination, the deadened hearts, of English women.

Love, whether it manifests on a wide national scale, or in the individual life, is a harmonious working of feeling, thought, and will. Until society as a whole has learnt to feel the Christ-Impulse, and think the Christ-Concept, it cannot hope to carry out the Christ-Will. All efforts to pass from Faith directly to will, without the intermediary step of thought, have so far proved abortive in the long run : there is plenty of evidence to show this, from the failure of the Franciscan Order onwards.

It is when one dwells on this third stage, the descent of the Christ-Impulse into the will, that the Symbol of the Holy Grail rises before the mind. For the blood is, according to Steiner's teaching, the only part of man's physical body which, at this stage of his evolution, can act as the physical basis of his own individual will : the rest of his body is still the Temple, in which work spiritual Beings far loftier than man himself.

But the blood of Jesus of Nazareth was not the bearer of his individual will : it was, together with the rest of his body, a purified vessel into which the Will of Christ could descend.

The blood of the man of our Fifth Epoch is so organised that it must be, to a lesser or a greater degree, the bearer of his *own* will : the Englishman especially has this power—the greater his Ego, the more completely does he "fill" his blood. In so far as his own Ego is filled with the Christ-Impulse, he has a special power of manifesting this Impulse by action in the objective world. But his blood cannot become the bearer of an Ego more advanced than his own, or of a direct Impulse from the spiritual world.

In his lectures on the Gospel of St. Matthew, Rudolf Steiner refers to two distinct types of Initiate :

"Those who were initiated into the secrets of the Mysteries were divided into certain classes, and they approached these secrets in several different ways. Some were instructed more in the way in which external man should live, what the outer man should accomplish, that he might fit himself to be a temple for the descending Sun-Spirit. And there were other pupils of the Mysteries, whose attention was more especially directed towards that which the soul must develop in silence within itself, if it wishes to arrive at understanding, feeling and experiencing a Sun-Spirit. Can you not imagine that it was natural that there were some pupils of the Mysteries whose task it was so to direct their outer life, on which the greatest care had been expended from earliest childhood, that their body should be able to follow a path of evolution which would enable them to become vehicles—temples, for a descending Sun-Spirit ? This happened in ancient times, and in reality it also happens in modern times, only it is not noticed amidst the external materialistic outlook of to-day."

Rudolf Steiner stresses the great importance of the fact that the Descent of Christ to the physical plane will *never* be repeated : it was a macrocosmic Deed, the central point of the whole earth-evolution. He teaches that Christ will, in the near future, become visible in the spiritual world to those who seek Him : but to suggest that Christ Himself will again descend into matter is to destroy the whole foundation of esoteric Christianity. Nevertheless, mighty Sun-Spirits, who are the divine Servants of Christ, can bear new Impulses from their Leader into the physical plane : and Christ Himself now dwells in the spiritual plane nearest to man.

The descent of a Christ-Impulse into the physical plane would not mean that man had reached the crown and summit of his earthly activity ; but it would mean that for a space of time man could "rest" in the state of balance, the love, he had himself created. In such a period of blissful consummation countless human beings would advance in their own personal evolution. What the human race creates in such periods is passed on as a heritage to future generations ; it is never lost, although man is destined to ascend again, through strife and anguish, to ever greater heights.

The Holy Grail is a Symbol for the purified human blood which can become the bearer of Divine Will : it became the Image of the highest earthly mission of the Celt in Christian times. For the Celt retained the unmixed blood of the pre-Christian races. His blood was not adapted to be the bearer of his individual will : but, when purified by the Ego, from within, of all racial taint—in the widest possible sense of the word—it could become an earthly image of the sacred Blood of the Grail : it could become a vessel into which an Impulse from the Spiritual world could for a time incarnate, in such a way that it could manifest as will, in action, on the physical plane— bringing about deeds greater than man himself could compass without divine help. Such help would only be vouchsafed at moments of time when man's own Ego was too weak to struggle against the Powers of Evil, here on the material plane—when indeed he was in danger of being overwhelmed by Satanic forces far stronger than himself.

Wagner, in his opera "Lohengrin" gives in artistic form a conception of such a divine Helper. These are the words in which the Swan-Knight describes himself and his mission :

"A distant land, where none may come unbidden,
    Holdeth a castle, Monsalvat 'tis named ;
    within its walls standeth a temple hidden . . .
    There is enshrined a treasured gift from heaven,
    a Cup that wondrous miracles hath wrought,
    which once, for mortal's adoration given,
    a troop of holy angels thither brought.
    Once every year a Dove from heaven descendeth,
    its magic power to strengthen and renew ;
    'tis called the Grail, and purest faith it sendeth
    to bless its band of knights devout and true.
    He whom the Grail as loyal servant chooseth—

undaunted is his heart, resistless his arm ;
on him all evil craft its power loseth,
before him, e'en death gives way and dares not harm.
Haply may he to far-off lands betake him,
as guardian true of virtue's right alone ;
but yet will not the holy Grail forsake him,
if, as its knight, he there abides unknown.
Such sacred mysteries the Grail containeth,
that veiled it must be held from mortal eye ;
in every knight your trust its rule ordaineth ;
if known his name, from you he straight must fly.
Now, hear, thus am I forced to tell my story !
The Grail sent me to you, to guard the right.
My father, Parsifal, reigns there in glory ;
To you I came, as Lohengrin, his knight."

Lohengrin appears at a moment when the German peoples are in danger of being overwhelmed by the Huns, who are pressing on their Eastern borders. He is prepared to lead them against their foes, to defend them with his invincible sword : to manifest his power as will on the earth plane, in concrete earthly deeds.

But before he can become the Guardian of Brabant, before the divine Impulse he bears can pass into the will, it must first permeate the feminine principles, as every true Ego-thought must do before it can become action. This permeation of the feminine principles— the astral and etheric bodies—is symbolised by the marriage of Lohengrin with Elsa : he can only work if the feminine principles are strong and pure enough to play their part. The men of the nation must enter into activity, must fight with the sword of the Ego around their Leader, while the women must become as the purified Cup which holds the Blood. A Christ-Impulse cannot manifest on earth as Love through will alone, but only through a harmonious inter-play of thought, feeling, and will. Lohengrin rescues Elsa from her foes, but he cannot perform his objective task except in conjunction with her : when she fails him, his work on earth is frustrated. The Swan which has brought him does not bear him back to the spiritual world from which he has come, for Wagner delicately conveys the impression that Lohengrin's "bearer," is a human being, Elsa's brother, the young Duke Gottfried. A high spiritual Impulse might have worked through this youthful ruler had his people been able to recognise and accept it, but the change which had come over the boy as the result of his being prepared to "receive" a higher Being had apparently altered his whole nature, in a way inexplicable to those in his environment. It was this "drowning" of Gottfried's own personality which aroused such alarm and anger in those who were unable to grasp what was happening. Elsa, his sister-soul, the representative of her people, can bear the strain of losing the familiar personality of her brother, having received a message from the spiritual world which has given her faith in him. But when the miracle has happened she cannot refrain from insisting on a detailed explanation of how the Spiritual Impulse has possessed him. She is not content to recognise and accept the manifestation of Divine Love vouchsafed to her : she wastes her strength in demanding knowledge for which she is not ripe—knowledge in advance of what has been freely given to mankind in her day. She will not win conviction by prolonged, silent meditation on the facts she has herself perceived :

she demands to be told, in exact terms, the nature and the source of the Spiritual Guidance sent to Brabant. As a result she—and, through her, the people—drive away the higher Being from the physical body through which it could have worked.

Gottfried returned to the normal life of his day : but that part of his Soul which had united with Lohengrin perished—his Spiritual Soul died with Elsa. The enemies of Christian Germany could not be completely conquered—only held at bay on her borders.

An even more remarkable picture of the Grail-Initiate is to be found in Tennyson's poems, "The Coming of Arthur" and "The Passing of Arthur." From his twenty-sixth year till almost the end of his long life Tennyson's mind hovered round the story of Arthur. There is evidence that he wished to create an epic dealing with the subject at full length : he began to write "Morte d'Arthur" in 1834, and the last of the Idylls—"Balin and Balan"—was published in 1885. In his main object Tennyson failed : indeed it is doubtful whether, in the nineteenth century, any language would have lent itself to the expression of a theme so inwoven with mystical experience : music was a far more fitting medium. Nevertheless, in the two poems mentioned, and also in "The Holy Grail," Tennyson's treatment of the figure of Arthur has remarkable simplicity, clarity and strength : these poems give the impression of a series of Imaginative pictures, brought down into materialisation by the force of the English language, which through its very nature can only deal with spiritual matters by densifying them, bringing them down to the plane of earth, where their spiritual nature is none the less real because, like the crystal, it is enshrined in physical forms.

One is driven to what some readers might consider a fantastic conclusion—that Arthur himself in actuality entered more deeply into the physical plane than any of his knights, who to Tennyson remained shadowy, unreal figures, their spiritual reality perpetually eluding his grasp : indeed, the whole subject remained outside his grasp, in spite of life-long efforts to seize it, except the part that concerned the Coming and the Passing of the King himself. These two poems, imperfect as they are, may prove to contain something very precious for the English people : they certainly contain a remarkable confirmation of the Christian teaching of Rudolf Steiner. The fact that Tennyson was so drawn to the figure of Arthur, and the particular manner in which he selected and treated the material available, are as significant for the English people as Wagner's choice and treatment of the theme of Parsifal is for the Germans.

King Lear, whom, through Shakespeare, we recognise as the great Protagonist of the Spiritual Soul, belonged to Celtic Britain. Rudolf Steiner teaches us that the land in which a nation works out its destiny is closely connected with its powers of soul and spirit, and in spite of the apparent break in the history of this land, Shakespeare felt an inner spiritual connection between the Celtic Britons and those who afterwards came to build up the England we know. Arthur himself is the living bond between the Britons and the English.

After the withdrawal of the Roman Legions which had held them together in artificial unity, the Celts in Britain fell into hopeless discord, broken and divided among petty kings whose fierce internecine strife destroyed the illusory peace that Rome had preserved by force; while at the same time the Germanic warriors began to pour into the land, taking advantage of the disunion which prevailed.

> "And so there grew great tracts of wilderness,
> Wherein the beast was ever more and more,
> But man was less and less, till Arthur came."

The legends concerning the birth of Arthur suggest that he was a dual being; the bearer of an Ego not his own.

His people were asked by Merlin to accept him as the posthumous son of King Uther, and Ygerne, widow of the Cornish prince Gorlois, whom he had married against her will, immediately after slaying her husband. Uther died, "moaning and wailing for an heir," on the very night of Arthur's birth, which, being premature, made it doubtful whether he was the son of Uther or the son of Gorlois. Moreover, the Queen was afraid to entrust her son to the fierce lords of Uther :

> "Wild beasts, and surely would have torn the child
> Piecemeal among them, had they known; for each
> But sought to rule for his own self and hand . . ."

She delivered him to Merlin, "to be holden far apart, Until his hour should come." He was reared by Sir Anton, an old knight, who was also thought by some to be his father.

This legend implies that Arthur's blood was pure of that racial principle which had become the evil genius of the Celt. He did not reign by right of descent from the father; for when Merlin finally brought him forth, his great lords refused to acknowledge him:

> "A hundred voices cried, 'Away with him!'
> No king of ours!   A son of Gorlois he,
> Or else the child of Anton, and no king,
> Or else baseborn."

He is finally accepted because of his mighty deeds in battle.

> "Sir and my liege . . . the fire of God
> Descends upon thee in the battle-field:
> I know thee for my King!"

But to Bellicent, a daughter of Ygerne and Gorlois, the ancient sage Bleys, the master of Merlin himself, entrusted still another account of Arthur's birth. He described how he and Merlin, on the night of the birth, at Tintagel, beheld approaching the castle a mysterious ship; in shape, "a dragon wing'd."

> ''And all from stem to stern
> Bright with a shining people on the decks,
> And gone as soon as seen."

Descending to the cove, they beheld eight great waves roll shoreward:

> "Till last, a ninth one, gathering half the deep,
> And full of voices, slowly rose and plunged
> Roaring, and all the wave was in a flame:
> And down the wave and in the flame was borne
> A naked babe, and rode to Merlin's feet,

Who stoopt and caught the babe, and cried, 'The King !
Here is an heir for Uther !'   And the fringe
Of that great breaker, sweeping up the strand,
Lash'd at the wizard as he spake the word,
And all at once all round him rose in fire,
So that the child and he were clothed in fire.
And presently thereafter follow'd calm,
Free sky and stars : 'And this same child,' he said,
'Is he who reigns ; nor could I part in peace
Till this were told.'"

When Bellicent questioned Merlin about this story,
he would give only "a riddling answer" :

"From the great deep to the great deep he goes."

But Merlin, nevertheless, declared in earnest to the
wondering knights :

"Tho' men may wound him . . . he will not die,
But pass, again to come ; and then or now
Utterly smite the heathen underfoot."

A passage in "The Holy Grail" suggests that Arthur
was aware of himself as the bearer of a Being far more
powerful than his own Individuality : that he was,
indeed, an earthly image of the Grail.

His knights, attracted by the Quest, leave the service
of the Round Table, to search for the mystic Cup,
which perpetually eludes them.   Arthur warns them
sadly that their quest will be vain, and when at length
many of them return, he addresses them thus :

"And spake I not too truly, O my knights ?
Was I too dark a prophet when I said
To those who went upon the Holy Quest,
That most of them would follow wandering fires,
Lost in the quagmire ?—lost to me and gone,

And left me gazing at a barren board,
And a lean Order—scarce returned a tithe—
And out of those to whom the vision came
My greatest hardly will believe he saw ;
Another hath beheld it afar off,
And leaving human wrongs to right themselves,
Cares but to pass into the silent life . . .
And some among you held, that if the King
Had seen the sight, he would have sworn the vow :
Not easily, seeing that the King must guard
That which he rules, and is but as the hind
To whom a space of land is given to plow.
Who may not wander from the allotted field
Before his work be done ; but, being done,
Let visions of the night or of the day
Come, as they will ; and many a time they come,
Until this earth he walks on seems not earth,
This light that strikes his eyeball is not light,
This air that smites his forehead is not air
But vision—yea, his very hand and foot—
In moments when he feels he cannot die,
And knows himself no vision to himself,
Nor the high God a vision, nor that One
Who rose again : ye have seen what ye have seen."

This passage suggests that the mission of the Grail-Initiate is connected with the manifestation of will, in action on the material earth. The descent of the higher Ego into Arthur's purified, ego-less blood is symbolised by his receiving the sword Excalibur. He himself has no sword ; out of his own power he does not even know whether he may accept the sword which rises mysteriously out of the Lake, for the words "Take me" are engraved on it in "the oldest tongue of all the world"—a language which only Merlin can read. But the words "Cast me away,"

Arthur can read easily, and he is preparing to cast the weapon back into the lake when Merlin forbids him to do this :

> " 'Take thou and strike ! the time to cast away
>   Is yet far off.'   So this great brand
>   The king took, and by this will beat his foemen down."

This passage shows clearly that Arthur himself had no craving for power : that the power he possessed in the outer world did not emanate from himself. Excalibur was the symbol of a Will, not his own, united with his blood, striking with his arm.

It is necessary to connect with this passage the legend of the Passing of Arthur. He is saved from death because, by an act of his own individual will, he gives up the power that has worked through him. He casts away Excalibur, and by that deed he remains living. Spiritual powers connected with the Soul : "three Queens with crowns of gold"—the feminine principles—receive the pure body of the King, and cherish it in a secret part of his realm : for at some future time the blood of Arthur will again become the bearer of a Spiritual Impulse : again Excalibur will be placed in those hands which have been strong enough to cast it away.

At the time of his crowning, Arthur has already received Excalibur, and round him gather a small band of faithful knights who, entirely of their free will, moved by no outer compulsion, cry :

> "Be thou the king, and we will work thy will,
>   Who love thee."

Arthur then forms them into his new Order :

> "Then the King in low deep tones,
>   And simple words of great authority,
>   Bound them by so strait vows to his own self,
>   That when they rose, knighted from kneeling, some
>   Were pale as at the passing of a ghost,
>   Some flush'd, and others dazed, as one who wakes
>   Half-blinded at the coming of a light."

But although the king is now the bearer of a powerful Ego : although he has his sword Excalibur : although he has, in his Round Table, a perfect instrument of his will : although he has the aid of divine Soul Powers, and of the Lady of the Lake, who seems to represent a pure etheric force—yet he cannot begin his mission till he has united himself with the human feminine principles. He beholds Guinevere, and recognises in her the highest representative of the people he has come to serve. She is "fairest of all flesh on earth." Until he can unite with her, he is unable to use the power dwelling within him, he is "vext with waste dreams."

> "For saving I be joined
>   To her that is the fairest under heaven,
>   I seem as nothing in the mighty world,
>   And cannot will my will, nor work my work
>   Wholly, nor make myself in mine own realm
>   Victor and lord. But were I join'd with her,
>   Then might we live together as one life,
>   And reigning with one will in everything,
>   Have power on this dark land to lighten it,
>   And power on this dead world to make it live."

Arthur himself can only provide for the indwelling Ego the purified male element, the blood. But, since

the descent of Christ, no Ego, however exalted, can
be active on earth except by passing first through the
feminine principles. As Lohengrin cannot work
except through union with Elsa, so Arthur must
unite himself with Guinevere. The Cup is an
essential part of the Grail. The Folk-Soul of a people
is expressed most strongly in the women, so that the
marriage of the King symbolises his union with the
nation he rules and serves.

Like Lohengrin, Arthur has first to rescue his bride
from deadly peril : the fight for Guinevere is the first
battle in which he uses Excalibur :

> "The Powers who walk the world
> Made lightnings and great thunders over him,
> And dazed all eyes . . ."

The Will-Initiate is King, not Priest : he cannot
express himself except in and through his people.
His union with Guinevere marks the beginning of his
constructive work on earth.

> "And holy Dubric spread his hands and spake,
> ' Reign ye, and live and love, and make the world
> Other, and may thy Queen be one with thee,
> And all this Order of thy Table Round
> Fulfil the boundless purpose of their King.' "

United with the purest essence of his people, Arthur
overcomes all factions, drives back the heathen,
wrests his country from the dying grasp of Rome, and
establishes for a brief space on earth an image of the
Holy Jerusalem. His people freely acknowledge in
him their spiritual Head.

"Strike for the King and live ! his knights have heard
That God hath told the King a secret word . . .

"Blow trumpet ! he will lift us from the dust.
Blow trumpet ! live the strength and die the lust . . .

"The King will follow Christ, and we the King
In whom high God hath breathed a secret thing.
Fall battleaxe, and flash brand !   Let the King reign."

Lohengrin is unable to work at all on earth, since
Elsa fails him at the very beginning of her task, the
Soul of the people proving itself too weak to act as
the Cup.   Arthur's reign is brief, because in Guinevere
the inveterate nature-instincts of the Celtic race revive,
spreading rapidly through the circle of knights,
expressing themselves as lust and strife.   The King
can no longer hold together his Round Table, and
finally his nephew Modred, son of Lot, King of the
Orkneys, makes a treacherous pact with the invading
heathen.   In the last great battle, all the knights save
Bedivere are slain, and Arthur, having received a
mortal wound in killing the traitor Modred, lies dying,
conscious of failure, yet aware that at some future
time he will resume his earthly mission :

"All my realm
Reels back into the beast, and is no more.
My God, thou hast forgotten me in my death :
Nay—God my Christ—I pass but shall not die."

By a last act of will, Arthur flings away Excalibur,
the symbol of the strength which is not his own,
renouncing utterly and completely, out of his own
Ego, this divine strength.   Yet it is significant that
the physical action of hurling Excalibur into the

Lake is done by the reluctant Bedivere : the King's individual Ego works only in his thought, issuing as a command—it is never expressed directly as will in his physical body. What remained when he had renounced Excalibur was the earthly Arthur, the son of Ygerne.

Then comes the remarkable scene of his Passing : his still living body is received into a spiritual feminine element—the three fair Queens whom Bellicent had observed near his throne. But all the decks of the magic ship were "dense with stately forms" : Arthur did not die, he passed out of the Fourth Epoch into the Fifth, into a race that as yet did not exist on the physical earth. For only in the Fifth Epoch do the three Soul Powers—the Sentient Soul, the Intellectual Soul, and the Spiritual Soul—develop themselves in man.

The Passing of Arthur points to the secret of England : that she bears a two-fold physical element.

The blood of the Englishman is dynamic, the bearer of his individual will ; through this the Spiritual Soul in England finds its normal means of expression on the physical plane. But the English Folk-Soul may also be united, not with the Celtic race, which is passed on through the mother, but with the Celtic blood, an element transmitted through the father, when—and only when—that element can be kept free of all racial taint, all astral passions, and all evil occult influences : conditions comparatively rarely fulfilled.

Through this pure, receptive element—the blood of Lear, the blood of Arthur—England possesses the power to receive a Grail-Initiate, who can manifest the Will of God on earth with a force beyond what is possible to any human Ego at this stage of man's evolution. Through what has been transmitted to her by Celtic Britain, combined with her own highest, most conscious Soul-powers, England has the potentiality of becoming for a brief space of time, an earthly image of the Grail ; though clearly she is powerless to realise out of her own will this, her noblest, highest possibility.

Yet she does possess negative power—the power to frustrate the working of Divine Will. For unless the Spiritual Soul can purify and strengthen herself, she cannot reflect her Prototype, the sacred Cup. Only through humility, through willingness to permeate herself with the Christ-Thought, to receive it creatively in full consciousness, can she grow strong and pure. There is no other upward path for the Soul in the Fifth Epoch but the way that leads through conceptual thought of the loftiest type : all other paths lead downwards.

At this moment of time it may be said in all earnestness that the fate of the whole human race depends on there being a sufficient number of men and women —of women especially—willing and able to receive creatively the new Concepts that have been freely given from the Spiritual World—only to be rejected, or tossed aside indifferently and lazily by human beings who seem blind and deaf to the evil destructive forces that are daily gathering momentum, and cannot fail to break like a great tidal wave over the earth if they are not strongly countered by an active, positive will for Good ; mere passive wishing for Good is useless. Before England can will, she must feel, and illumine her feeling with thought. If England would save herself and the world, let her begin now the task of purification by thought : so that at least she may be prepared, should the Divine Will so ordain, to serve as an earthly image of the holy Vessel—for without the co-operation of Man, God's Will cannot be done on earth :

> "O living Will, that shalt endure
>   When all that seems shall suffer shock,
>   Rise in the spiritual rock,
> Flow through our deeds and make them pure.